Every House Tells a Story

A History of Some of Langford's Older Houses
and the People Who Lived in Them

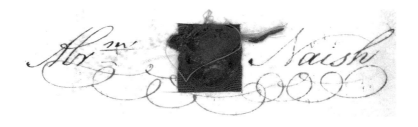

The Langford History Group

www.langfordhistory.com

Reprinted in 2009 with minor changes

First published in 2006
by The Langford History Group
www.langfordhistory.com

Cover designed by Stefan Marjoram
House photos by Stefan Marjoram
Edited by Jo Fryer, John Gowar, Jill Hale, Liz Hyde and Alex Kolombos
Typeset by Max Kolombos

printed and bound by
The European Print Group, New Bond Street, London

ISBN 978-0-9562253-0-6

Also available from The Langford History Group:

  More Stories From Langford - History and Tales of Houses and Families

Contents

Colour Plate Contents

Introduction

Old houses may hold many secrets and it can be fascinating to research their history and reveal their stories. Some of Langford's houses can be dated back to the Stuart age, particularly the Jacobean years of the 17th century. Others were built in Georgian, Victorian and Edwardian times.

Most of Langford's houses have been built from the local limestone and some have been rendered and colour washed. All have the impression of being well cared for and give the village a prosperous feel.

For such a small village Langford has a large number of fine old country houses, originally built for the gentry, such as Langford House, Langford Place and Langford Court. Also it is evident that a large number of new houses were being constructed during the 1820s. Was this the influence of Langford Court or could it have had something to do with the merchants from Bristol wishing to move out from the increasingly polluted town to the cleaner, greener climate to be found in the foothills of the Mendips? With the turnpike road in place it would have only been a 2 hour coach ride into Bristol, so the merchants would have been able to keep an eye on their affairs while enjoying the rural delights of the village.

Census returns are released when 100 years have passed and originate from the beginning of the 19th century. The earliest complete census dates from 1841. The first census lists the inhabitants in each house, their occupations and place of birth. Subsequent ones give occupations as well and many people in Langford are listed as agricultural workers, gardeners, housemaids, dairymaids, dressmakers, glove makers, cordwainers (shoe makers), coachmen, grooms and cooks and would have been employed in the big houses such as Somerlea, Hylsbroke/Milfort, Maysmead Place, Langford House, Langford Place and Langford Court.

There are also many cottages in Langford, some of which were connected to its former tanning industry which appears to have been in operation at various sites from the 1400s to the mid 1800s. Many of the cottages were occupied by tenants, several of whom would have worked for the owners of the larger houses, or on the land as agricultural labourers.

The cottages were usually built as '2 up and 2 down' properties, often with a lean-to for jobs like boiling clothes and salting meat. They would have had an outside 'privvy' and in the garden there would possibly have been a pigsty as well as a coop for hens. Some of the households would have shared a pump for their water supply whilst others had their own well on their property. Today although many of the cottages have been extended, it is often possible to identify the original core from clues such as thick stone walls, inglenooks, beams and old doors.

It was not customary for even the grand houses in Langford to be built with cellars. This was for a very good reason. Langford is not many feet above sea level and the Langford Brook flows through its centre. This flows into the river Yeo, which in turn flows into the sea between Weston super Mare and Clevedon. The latter part of the Yeo is tidal, which can affect the water table higher up, if there is a period of exceptionally heavy rain coinciding with a high tide. Consequently cellars could be prone to flooding.

It is interesting to look at how people used to live at different times in the history of Langford's houses. What jobs did the inhabitants have? How large were their families? How long did they live? Did they move to different properties within Langford? The researchers have endeavoured to answer some of these questions with the help of the census data and reminiscences of some of our older residents.

Several early Somerset maps have been included which reveal tantalising glimpses of the village's development. These clearly show the ford which gave rise to the village's name and which even till present times divides Langford between the parishes of Burrington and Churchill.

This book has come about as a result of the hard work of many of the members of the Langford History Group who have given a lot of their time to researching the history of the houses which appear in this book.

It is hoped that people who read this book will enjoy the opportunity to gain a greater insight into Langford's many and varied old houses and that maybe this will inspire others to research their own house.

Please feel free to visit our website at **www.langfordhistory.com** where you can view and participate in our continuing efforts to research our village's history.

Position of Langford

The village of Langford is situated 12 miles south-west from Bristol and 8 miles east of Weston-super-Mare. It is north of the Mendip Hills, which are close by.

At one time, the main turnpike road passed through the centre of the village, but in 1932 a by-pass was completed and this now forms part of the busy A38.

And interesting and unusual feature of the village is that it has grown up across the boundary of two parishes and the two medieval manors of Wrington and Glastonbury. Today the village is still split into two parishes, depending on which side of the Langford Brook the property is sited. Those on the east side are in the parish of Burrington and those on the west are in Churchill parish.

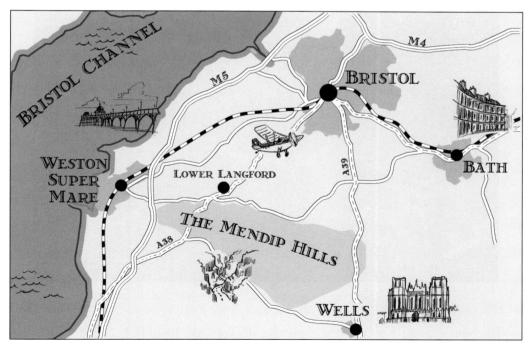

Map showing Langford in relation to Bristol and Weston-super-Mare

Aerial view showing Langford Road, Blackmoor and the by-pass
(See Colour Plate 1, Page 111)

The houses researched are sited along the old Turnpike Road from Langford Place in the east, to Langford House in the west, as well as properties in Blackmoor. Langford Court in Langford Lane has also been included.

Langford in Maps

John Gowar

Although care has to be taken in drawing inferences from old maps, Langford has featured on many that have been published over more than three centuries. Maps that are sufficiently detailed for the development of individual properties to be followed start with the tithe maps from around 1840.

Background

The earliest of the county atlases of England is that of Christopher Saxton. His map of Somerset is dated 1575 but Langford is not shown on it. As he travelled the country, Saxton carried with him an official letter instructing that he be conducted *unto any tower, castle, high place or hill* to view the surrounding region. The accuracy he achieved indicates some primitive form of triangulation, but his maps showed no roads. They nevertheless formed the basis of almost all the maps of English counties that were published over the following 200 years. Later cartographers added and altered names, showed roads and hundred boundaries, and embellished their maps in numerous individual ways, but the basic structure remained unaltered. They were redrawn rather than re-surveyed and Langford is shown on many of them. The English County maps of Emanuel Bowen, in particular, have much written and illustrative detail. In 1725, John Strachey of Sutton Court produced a large map of Somerset in this style, with a border showing the coats of arms of local gentry. It was intended to accompany his *History of Somerset*. The map was printed but the history remained unpublished. The manuscript notes for it are held at Somerset Record Office.

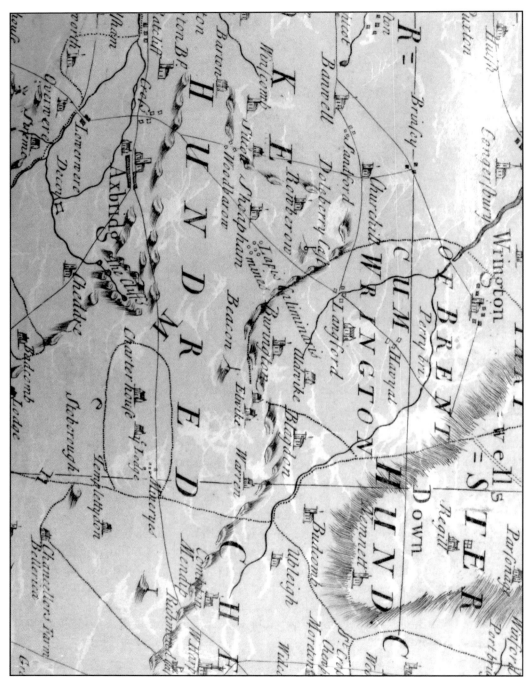

Part of John Strachey's map of Somerset, 1725, showing the area around Langford.
(Courtesy of Somerset Record Office)

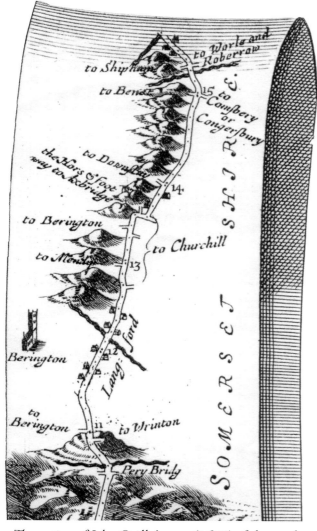

The first cartographic reference to Langford known to the author is that on John Ogilby's linear road map of 1675. This was entitled *Continuation of the Road from London to Bristol ... Continued to Huntspil* and his representation of the part that ran through Langford is shown in the figure.

The section of John Ogilby's map (1675) of the coach road from Bristol that ran through Langford.

In 1769, Benjamin Donn published a map of *Bristol and 11 miles around* at a scale of about 0.7 miles to the inch. It just extends to Langford, which is shown with houses on either side of the main road. Donn was Principal of the Mathematical Academy in King's Street, Bristol and by 1790, when he published a similar map of the country 11 miles around Bath, he had taken to styling himself Donne. His maps were drawn from detailed surveys made using the sophisticated techniques and improved instruments that had been developed in the eighteenth century. However, he attempted no survey of the whole of Somerset. That was left to William Day and his apprentice surveyor, Charles Masters, and was carried out between 1775 and 1782. Their map was published in nine sheets, at a scale of approximately one mile to the inch. In all three of these maps, Ogilby, Donn and Day & Masters, the portrayal of individual properties in Langford has to be assumed to be schematic.

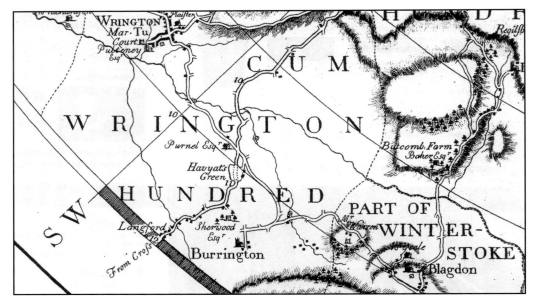

Langford as shown on Benjamin Donn's map of 11 miles around Bristol, 1769

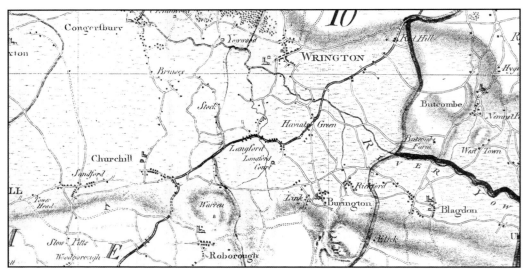

Langford as shown on Day and Masters' map of Somerset, 1786

The First Ordnance Survey, the Turnpike and the Commutation of Tithes

Making detailed inferences from old maps is an exercise that is fraught with difficulty. It is necessary to be sure about when and how the original survey was carried out, whether the map was compiled from that original survey or has been altered subsequently, and whether such alterations were made to correct errors, to add information, or to update for changes that had occurred on the ground. Alterations may not be documented and may also have introduced errors. With this health-warning in mind, we have reached the time from which printed maps can tell us about the way Langford properties have developed over nearly two centuries.

The early 19th century saw the first results of the comprehensive and contiguous survey of the whole country conducted by the Ordnance Survey. The area around Langford was surveyed about 1807 and copies exist of the surveyors' draft drawings, which were made at a scale of half a mile to the inch. These maps allow some larger properties to be distinguished with confidence for the first time, as can be seen from the illustration. They were published in 1817 at the scale of one mile to the inch and are known as the *Old Series*. Sheet 19 covers Langford.

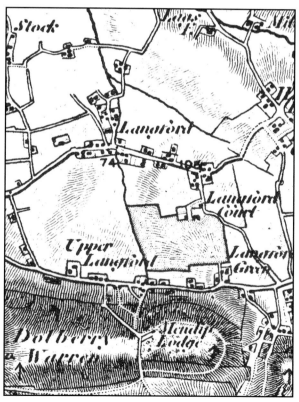

Part of the Old Series Ordnance Survey map of the area around Langford.

In 1818, a detailed plan was drawn giving details of the intended widening of the Bristol to Bridgwater turnpike. A copy is held at the Somerset Record Office. The representation of individual houses is schematic and incomplete but the accompanying schedule tells us the owners and occupiers of the seven properties in Langford that were to be affected. It would appear that No. 32 is Wistaria House and No. 33 is York Cottage.

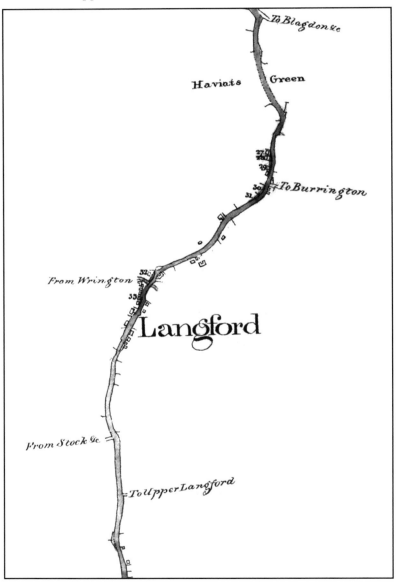

Part of the plan of the Bristol to Bridgwater turnpike road made in 1818, showing the
properties that would be affected by proposed improvements.
The owner and occupier of each of the plots are given in the table.
(See Colour Plate 2, Page 112) (Courtesy of Somerset Record Office)

		Owner	Occupier
27	Yard and Garden	John Lane	John Lane
28	Garden	Thomas Parker Jnr	Thomas Parker Jnr
29	Garden and Orchard	William Badman	William Badman
30	Orchard	Thomas Parker Snr	Thomas Parker Snr
31	Orchard and Garden	John Parker	John Parker
32	Garden	John Naish	James Fry
33	Court and Railing	Mr Edwards	James Weeks

Between 1836 and 1860, Parliament passed a number of Tithe Commutation Acts which were intended to make general and permanent the complex system of tithe payments that were previously local and temporary. All tithes, whatever their origin and whoever their recipient, were commuted into a tithe rent charge that was fixed in quantity of wheat, barley and oats, but paid in cash and so could vary in monetary value. Commissioners were appointed to execute the acts in each parish. Landholdings were individually numbered and shown on large-scale parish plans drawn especially for this purpose. The tithe maps for Langford are the earliest reliable cartographic record to show the position of identifiable individual properties in the village, other than those few just mentioned that were affected by the turnpike alterations.

Property in Langford falls into three parishes: Burrington, Churchill and Wrington, so there are three tithe apportionment Schedules and three maps.

The apportionments were drawn up as follows:

Parish	Date of Apportionment Agreement	Valuers	Recipient of Tithes
Burrington	21 March 1838	Haviland John Addington (Langford Court) James Cockburn (Wrington) James Stallard (Schoolmaster of Burrington)	Rev. John Vane (as Perpetual Curate of Burrington and Rector of Wrington)
Churchill	14 February 1842	William Body (South Brent) Joseph Edwards (Hutton)	John Fisher (* see below)
Wrington	16 June 1838	Robert Baker (Wrington) James Cockburn (Wrington) Charles Knowles (Wrington) John Bennett (Wrington) John Young (Broadfield)	Rev. John Vane (as Rector of Wrington)

John Fisher of Langford House held a lease of the appropriated tithes in Churchill from the Dean and Chapter of the Collegiate Church of the Holy and Indivisible Trinity in Bristol.

The areas of some of the landholdings, together with their owner and occupier, as detailed in the Schedules, are given in the tables on the following pages. The areas are given in acres, roods and perches. A perch (technically a square perch) was 30¼ square yards and a rood was 40 square perches. There were 4 roods to the acre.

This information can be correlated with the details of individual families recorded in the 1841 Census. This was the first census to record such information. It was taken on 6th June, 1841, and so is reasonably contemporary with the tithe apportionment schedules. This often enables particular properties and the families occupying them at this period to be identified with some confidence.

The three maps have been adjusted for scale and orientation, and merged to make a single sheet. The author is grateful to Richard Dunn of Nempnett Thrubwell for his skill in achieving this.

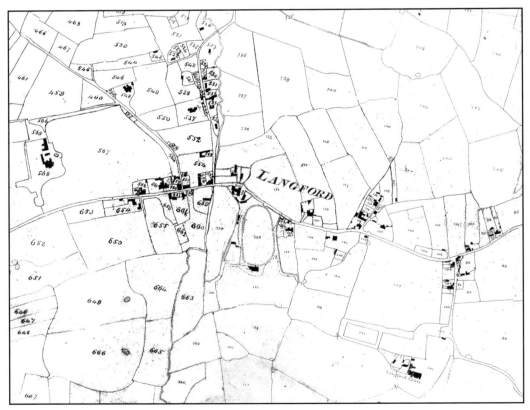

A composite map created by Richard Dunn from the three tithe apportionment maps for Burrington, Churchill and Wrington

Burrington Parish

No.	Landowner	Occupier	Description	Area			Current name
				acre	rood	pch	
106	Samuel Capper	Samuel Capper	Garden Offices etc	1	1	21	Langford Place
113	Thomas Brookman	Thomas Brookman Thomas Thorn	Tan Yard etc		3	18	Includes The Old Post Office
119 120	Joseph Lucas Lovell	Joseph Lucas Lovell	House & garden	3	0	17	Alden House (was Mendip Villa)
122 123	Abraham Naish	James Isgar	Orchard Garden	3 1	0 0	35 29	Wistaria House
125	John Fry & Isaac Cooper	Thomas Fenwick	Garden		2	6	Langford Inn
126 127	Reverend Thomas Jeffery Bumpsted	Reverend Thomas Jeffery Bumpsted	Garden Offices & Lawn	13	2	37	Milfort/ Hylsbroke
135a	Richard Burges	Beris Thiery	Garden			9	Nash House
136	Richard Burges	Richard Burges	Garden		1	11	Dring Cottage
137	Richard Burges	Robert Vicary James Hollier	Garden			11	Rose Cottage
140 141	James Kingcott	James Kingcott	Land	3	1	36	Lodge Farm
142	Robert Hacker	Robert Hacker	Garden			36	
147	Haviland John Addington	Haviland John Addington	Gardens etc	10	2	20	Langford Court

Churchill Parish

No.	Landowner	Occupier	Description	Area			Current name
				acre	rood	pch	
526	John Cook	William Counsell	House & Garden		3	6	
527	William Counsell	William Counsell	House & Garden	1	0	11	Sutledge House
528	Richard Burges	Richard Burges	Garden			25	

No.	Landowner	Occupier	Description	Area			Current name
				acre	rood	pch	
529	William Weeks	William Weeks	House & Garden			18	
530	Richard Burges	Samuel Derrick	House & Garden		1	4	
531	Matthew Tavernor	Samuel Andrews	Garden & House		1	5	
532	Thomas Parker Sr	Thomas Parker Sr	House Shop & Garden		1	0	
533	John Masters	John Masters	House & Garden			36	
534	Thomas Parker Jr	Thomas Parker Jr	House & Garden			28	
535	Job Harris	Job Harris	Garden & House			8	
536	William Paines	Richard Salter	House & Garden			13	
537	Joseph Wood	James Kingcott	House & Garden	1	1	13	Devonshire House
541	Henry Northover	Henry Northover	House & Garden			32	
543	Elizabeth Maria Armstrong	George Rowe	House & Garden			27	
548	Elizabeth Maria Armstrong	John Wilmot Bradford	House & Garden		2	0	Maysmead (Langford Cottage)
553	John Foster	James Badman etc	Houses & Gardens			28	Chapel (was Foster's Row)
555	Alexander Lane	Alexander Lane	House & Garden			15	Smithy
556	Charles Granger	Henry Pitman	Houses & Garden			29	(was Granger's Row)
557	Charles Granger	Thomas Reeves	House & Garden			24	
558	Charles Granger	Void	Cottage in ruins			10	
559	George Gane	Daniel Underwood	House & Garden			39	York Cottage
560	Sir John Tilden	Charlotte Synge	House & Garden		1	10	Richmond House
561	George Adams	Void	House & Garden		1	12	St Mary's House
562	John Fry	John Hill	House & Garden		1	0	Park Cottage
563	John Fry	Edward Davis	House & Garden			14	Attached to Park Cottage
568	John Fisher	John Fisher	House Garden & Lawn	3	1	39	Langford House

Large-scale Ordnance Survey Maps

The Old Series, one inch to the mile, Ordnance Survey maps were updated and reprinted throughout the 19th century. Among other revisions, the railway lines that were built subsequent to the initial survey are shown on many of the reprints currently available.

This area of Somerset was re-surveyed by the Ordnance Survey in 1882 and 1883, at the much larger scale of 1:2500, or 25.344 inches to the mile. From this survey, the *First Edition* large-scale maps were first published in 1885. Their detail and accuracy set a new cartographic standard. Roads were shown at their true width. Each field and enclosure was included with its precise boundaries, area and reference number. However, the boundaries of plots are not always identical with those shown on the tithe apportionment maps and the numbering is quite different.

In this area, the maps were redrawn at the reduced scale of six inches to the mile (1:10560), with the field reference numbers and areas omitted but with contour lines added at 50 ft. and 100 ft., and then at 100 ft. intervals. The survey was revised in 1902 and revised maps at the same scales were first published in 1903. These are known as the *First Revised Edition*.

The Ordnance Survey subsequently re-surveyed and revised its large-scale maps twice prior to the establishment of the National Grid. However, in this area, no maps from the Second Revision were published and of the Third Revision, the only maps to be issued were of the area south of a line passing through Langford House and the Chapel in Blackmoor. This was in 1931, so they included the new by-pass. A further revision, aligned with the National Grid was published for this area in 1975 and 1976. The Sheet Numbers are ST4660 and ST4661. Detailed topographical data is now held digitally in a national database.

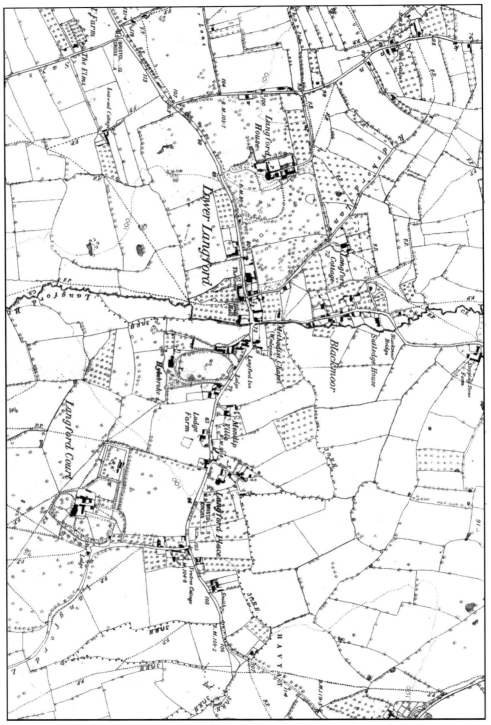

Ordnance Survey First Edition, Surveyed 1882/3, Printed 1885
Courtesy of Digimap: © Crown Copyright and Landmark Information Group Limited 2006

Ordnance Survey First Revision, Surveyed 1902, Printed 1904
Courtesy of Digimap: © Crown Copyright and Landmark Information Group Limited 2006

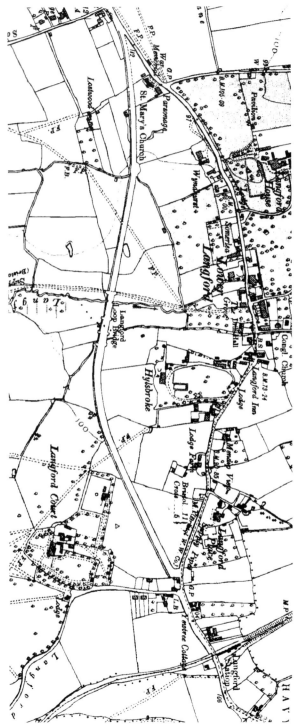

Ordnance Survey Third Revised Edition, Published 1931
Courtesy of Digimap: © Crown Copyright and Landmark Information Group Limited 2006

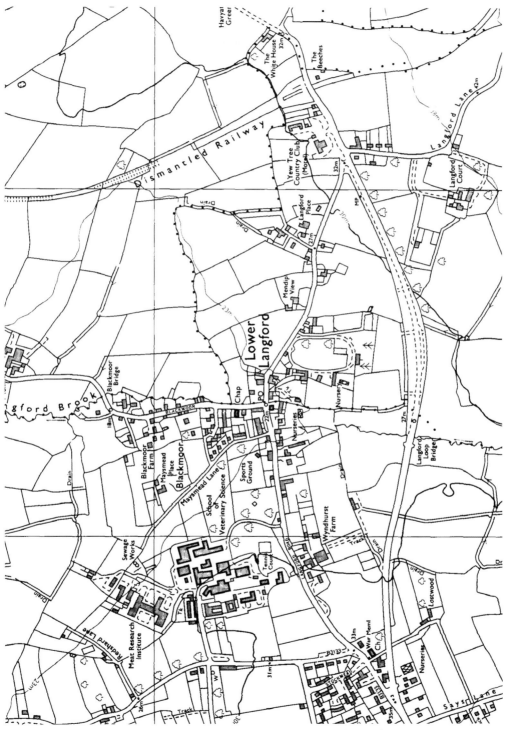

Ordnance Survey National Grid Edition, Published 1981
Courtesy of Digimap: © Crown Copyright and Landmark Information Group Limited 2006

House development in Langford from 1840 to the present day

A comparison between the tithe apportionment maps and the large-scale maps of 1885, 1903, 1931 and 1981 illustrates the way properties in the village have developed since the 1840s. Many houses have stood on the same site throughout this period, subject only to extensions and alterations. This applies to most of the houses described in this book.

In 1842, there were two tenement rows in Langford, each housing six or seven families of local workers. *Foster's Row*, No. 553 on the tithe map, was in Blackmoor on the site of the Chapel. *Granger's Row*, No. 556 on the tithe map, was on the Turnpike towards the east end of the site later to be used for the Victoria Jubilee Homes. Their eponymous owners were, respectively, John Foster and Charles Granger. Plot No. 555, on the corner of Blackmoor and the Turnpike, was then a smithy, although earlier documents indicate that it had previously been a tannery.

Between the 1840s and the 1880s, considerable building development occurred in Blackmoor. Several cottages and houses were demolished, several suffered extensive alteration and there was some new building. *Sutledge House* was expanded. The Chapel was built in 1846 on land donated by John Foster. Elsewhere, *Wistaria House* outbuildings are shown as having been extended to the road; the Mill has become the Drill Hall; both at *Somerlea* and at *The Grove*, previously separate buildings appear to have been linked; the tannery at Saxon Street has gone.

Two major developments that took place during the years between the 1880s and the 1900s were the building of the Victoria Jubilee Homes in 1887 and the construction of the Wrington Vale branch railway line to Blagdon which opened on 1st December, 1901. A comparison of the *First Edition* and the *Revised Edition* O.S. maps clearly illustrates these and other changes. In particular, there was further development in Blackmoor and the properties now called *The Bridge* and *Virginia Cottages* were built near the centre of the village. On the 1885 Ordnance Survey map, the Chapel is erroneously shown as *Methodist (Wesleyian)*, whereas in 1903, it is correctly described as *Congregational*.

The major development between 1903 and 1931 was the construction of the Langford by-pass in 1928. On the 1931 map, this is shown completed except for the final link to the turnpike road at the eastern end, where it is blocked by a cottage whose owner refused to sell. Within the village, *Roemarten* has been built between *The Grove* (now *The Forge*) and *Somerlea*. More recently, further alterations to property and new housing developments can be seen, especially in Maysmead (Redshard Lane), Blackmoor Close and Saxon Street.

Looking at a chronological sequence of maps in this way illustrates both the changes in the village and the development of map making. I wonder if other readers would agree that the modern digitally produced large-scale maps do, as yet, fall some way short of the cartographic elegance achieved by their predecessors of 100 years ago.

Sites of Houses in Langford

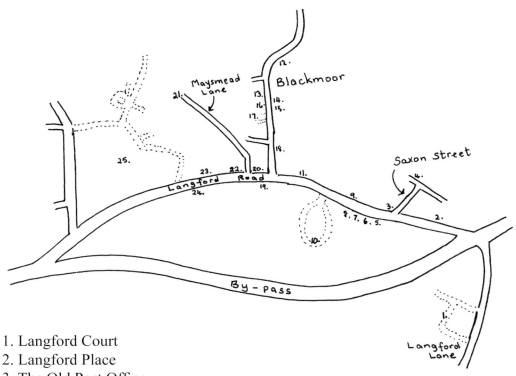

1. Langford Court
2. Langford Place
3. The Old Post Office
4. Laurel Cottage
5. Lodge Farm
6. Nash House
7. Rose Cottage, Burgesville
8. Dring Cottage
9. Alden House
10. Milfort/Hylesbroke
11. Wistaria House
12. Sutledge House
13. 1 Withey Cottages
14. Laurel House
15. Hopedale
16. Blackmoor Cottage
17. Devonshire House
18. Acacia House
19. The Hall
20. The Victoria Jubilee Homes
21. Maysmead Place
22. York Cottage
23. St Mary's House and Richmond House
24. Somerlea House
25. Langford House

-1-

Langford Court

Jo Fryer

Langford Court is believed to have existed in some form for over 400 years dating back to Elizabethan times. It has been occupied by many titled and famous people. It is believed to have first existed as a 'hunting seat'. During the 1940s and 1950s it was used by two different schools.

Langford Court is a listed building and is described as 'a detached house dated 1651 with early 19th century and 1875 alterations and additions.' The main building has two projecting wings of two storeys giving symmetry to the property. There is a date tablet above the fanlight showing 1651 and another date acknowledging the 1875 extension, above the clock. This two storey addition is lower than the main building and has mullion windows. The south facing elevation is the front of the house and looks towards the Mendips. It has a ha-ha to create the illusion of the fields being part of the garden. The rear of the original building has 17th century dormer windows.

The origins of Langford Court are thought to date back to the 1500s when a hunting lodge was used here by the Capell family, who bought the Manor of Wrington in 1546, following the dissolution of Glastonbury Monastery. The Mendips were a favoured hunting ground in Elizabethan times and this hunting seat gave access to the deer and wild boar that were in great abundance there.

A property on the site was next owned by Giles Hoby (1565 - 1626). His first wife, Elizabeth Paulet, was a cousin of Sir Henry Capell, who owned the Manor of Wrington, and the granddaughter of William Paulet, who became the first Marquis of Winchester and was Lord High Treasurer for 22 years until his death at a great age in 1572. Giles came from Hailes Abbey in Gloucestershire, matriculated to Trinity College, Oxford, in 1583, aged 18, and was a patron of the lutanist, John Dowland, who dedicated a galliard to him in 1604.

The title deeds date back to 1590 when Giles Hoby sold Langford Court to John Allot, who was the Lord Mayor of London. He died in office in 1591, but it was 7 years before the estate was sold to Edward Kenn in 1597. His son William Kenn inherited it on Edward's death.

William Kenn then sold to Francis Creswicke in 1636. He was a wealthy Bristol merchant who owned Hanham Court and a sumptuously furnished town house in Bristol. He was Sheriff of Bristol in 1628 and a mayor of the City of Bristol in 1645. On his death the property at Langford Court was passed to Francis's second son, John Creswicke.

John Creswicke had three daughters and his eldest daughter married Cadwallader Jones. Their oldest son John Jones was bequeathed Langford Court by his grandfather, John Creswicke.

John Creswicke
1617-1703

John Jones married Elizabeth Clark in 1704, a year after he had inherited Langford Court. He was a wealthy man through his inheritance from the Creswickes. Elizabeth's mother was heiress to Sutton Court and her father was Comptroller to the Royal Household, making Elizabeth an eligible bride. But they decided to elope, dashing from Langford Court on

John Jones and Elizabeth Clark
1679-1737 1683-1712

Mrs Turner
1669-1749

horseback, with Elizabeth riding pillion, having made all their plans and preparation from a small room at Langford Court. John Jones kept a well stocked wine cellar for which he was renowned throughout the district.

A Mrs Turner was employed at Langford Court as housekeeper and worked there for forty six years. When John Jones died in 1737, his will stipulated that Mrs Turner should live at Langford Court until his son, Edward came of age. He also left her £200. He appointed her as an executrix 'in consideration of her time and faithful service to myself and children since'.

Edward Jones married Mary Musgrave and they had a daughter, Elizabeth Jane in 1740. In the same year Edward Jones set up a charity whereby thirteen pounds was to be made available annually for the poor of the parish of Burrington. Edward's sister, Mary, married John Somers of Regil, one of whose descendants, Mary Blanche Somers, was to return to live at Langford Court many years later.

When Edward Jones died, his daughter, Elizabeth, inherited Langford Court. She married John Withers Sherwood a barrister, who suffered a long and painful illness and died aged 34 in 1770. A white marble tablet commemorating him can be seen at Burrington Church.

Edward Jones
1711-1753

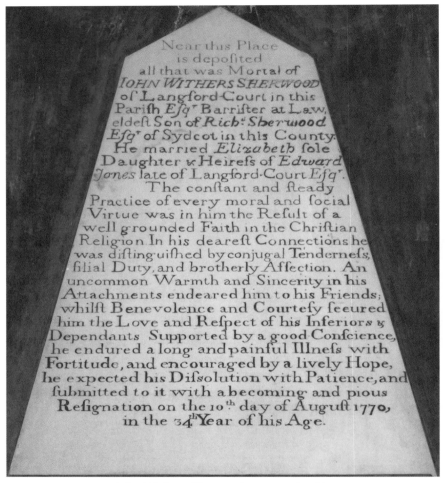

John Withers Sherwood memorial tablet

Elizabeth married again in 1774. Her second husband was the eccentric Reverend Thomas Sedgwick Whalley (1746 – 1828). Upon his marriage, Langford Court automatically became his and he set to work to modernise it. He began spending the fortune that had come his way and bought a house in the much sought after Royal Crescent at Bath and another in London.

Whilst living in Bath, Whalley was referred to as:

'a conspicuous figure in the set that fluttered around the spa squandering money in liberal hospitality.'

Whalley had been ordained in 1770. When he married at 27, he installed a curate in his rectory in Lincolnshire. He could now spend time writing poetry and plays and mixing with the famous and fashionable. Langford Court suited his needs better.

Revd. Whalley
1746-1828

Whalley entertained in all three of his properties and kept company with the famous Bath actress, Sarah Siddons and the lively diarist and novelist, Fanny Burney. When Fanny Burney met him she referred to him as:

> 'Immensely tall, thin and handsome, but affected, delicate and sentimentally pathetic.'

Whalley also socialised with distinguished people like Hannah More, Dr Johnson and William Wilberforce.

The city socialites enjoyed the rural pleasantries of Langford Court and in the summer months innumerable guests were invited.

Whalley's cousin, Sophie Weston, wrote to him saying:

> "It is a very holyday of my spirit to visit you, and Langford Court, my temple, my terrestrial paradise."

Whalley had built a reputation for lavish entertaining. The feasting, drinking, music, card playing and conversation would continue past midnight. One party had been brought to an end and the guests had called for their carriages only to find that a thick blanket of snow had covered the countryside. The roads were impassable as the drifts were several feet deep. Snow was still falling and any thoughts of returning home had to be abandoned. The guests would need to stay the night. The arctic conditions continued for a few more days and so did the party. Whalley fed his unexpected guests with mutton from the nearby sheep fold and they drank wine from his inexhaustible wine cellar.

In 1780 Whalley and his wife mortgaged Langford Court, 2 houses and approximately 270 acres of land comprising several fields and an orchard, to Robert Tucker for £3000.

Whalley was pleased with the enthusiasm people showed when coming to Langford Court to be entertained by him but by1783 he found it necessary to let Langford Court and live abroad. It was let to General Gunning in 1783 and 1786 to 1788, to Mrs. Aspinall in 1890, Henry Bosanquet Esq. from 1792 to 1796 and to the Rt. Hon. John Hiley Addington from 1797 to 1805.

In the meantime, in 1787, Whalley returned to England and decided to build what became a very stylish and lavish house which he called Mendip Lodge. It cost £60,000 to build and he took many of Langford Court's treasures to use in it, particularly the Adam fireplaces of marble and wood. It is thought that these were replaced when Mendip Lodge was knocked down.

He continued his spendthrift ways, spending both his money and his wife's fortune. The vast upkeep of his properties, including the numerous servants he employed, began to seriously eat into his funds. In 1782 the Whalleys mortgaged to Richard Lansdowne all the land previously mortgaged to Robert Tucker plus several fields for £6000.

Whalley and his wife lived in Mendip Lodge and in 1783 he let Langford Court to the General John Gunning who lived there with his wife and daughter. They lived there until 1788 when they moved to London.

General John Gunning was married to Susannah, a novelist who used her maiden name of Minifie as her pen name. Her books were sentimental, romantic fiction full of melodrama and high emotion and possibly similar to the Mills and Boon of today.

General Gunning had two sisters who were celebrated court beauties. In 1752 one of them, Elizabeth, married James, Duke of Hamilton after a whirlwind romance. Her wedding ring was taken from a bed curtain. Five years later James died and a year later, in 1756, Elizabeth married the Marquis of Lorne, soon to become the Duke of Argyel. Elizabeth had children by both her marriages, one of whom was the sixth Marquis of Lorne. Elizabeth, the Marquis's mother and Susannah, the General's wife, circulated reports and even forged a letter in the hope that an engagement would be engineered between Elizabeth, the Gunnings' only child (Elizabeth's niece) and the eligible Marquis

(Elizabeth's son) The match was to be made between the two cousins.

In the meantime, the Marquis of Blandford, the son of the Duke of Marlborough had been courting Elizabeth Gunning and she had told friends she was to be engaged to be married to him. General Gunning wrote to the Duke of Marlborough to find out about this match. A (forged) letter turned up at the Gunning's house, supposedly written by the Marquis of Blandford, releasing Elizabeth from any matrimonial promises. The letter was supposed to prompt the Marquis of Lorne's proposal. Cousins of General Gunning, Mr. and Mrs. Bowen then produced letters which were supposedly written by the General's daughter, Elizabeth, declaring her love for Lorne and not Blandford.

When General Gunning found out he was so indignant that he turned his wife and daughter out of his house. They were taken in by the Duchess of Bedford, grandmother of the original suitor, the Marquis of Blandford, who helped them find somewhere to live. The scandal hit the press and a parody of 'the House that Jack Built' made an amusing recital in many of the houses at the time.

This is the note
That was never read
This is the groom
That was never seen
To carry the note
That nobody read.
This is Minifie Gunning
Who used her cunning
The groom to prevent
That never was sent
This is the maiden all for Lorne,
Who now by her friends is tatter'd and torn
This is the General, somewhat too bold
Whose head was too hot, though his heart was too cold,
Who made himself single before it was meet,
And his wife and his daughter turned on to the street
To please the two Dukes
Whose serious rebukes
Frightened the Marquis shy of the horn
Who flew from the maiden all for Lorne
Who now by her friends is tatter'd and torn.

Susannah Gunning wrote an 'over the top' letter to the Duke of Argyll to declare her daughter's innocence, telling him that her daughter was an angel who was incapable of vice. She also accused her husband's 'evil' cousins, the Bowens, of forging letters.

The letter became public and the scandal was referred to as the 'Gunningiad' and in 1791 the caricaturist, James Gillray published some hand coloured etchings of the events which are now held in the National Portrait Gallery. One of them is called 'The Siege of Blenheim – or – the new system of gunning, discovered.'

But it would appear that General Gunning had also led a colourful life with many affairs and he was later exposed as an adulterer and fined £5,000 for 'criminal conversation' with his tailor's wife. He fled to Naples with his mistress. Susannah declared that she had regretted 22 out of 23 years of her marriage and as she is supposed to have based much of the content of her books on her private life, this probably gave her more material for her novels.

In 1797 the Rev. Whalley initially let and then in 1804 sold Langford Court for £6000 to the Rt. Hon. John Hiley Addington, who was the brother of the Prime Minister, Lord Sidmouth. John Hiley Addington was an M.P. and held government posts. He was Paymaster of the Forces in his brother's cabinet. He was patronage secretary to the Treasury, a position he hated, before becoming Lord of the Treasury. He was jealous of his brother, who was Prime Minister from 1801 to 1804, and was susceptible to gloom and hypochondria.

He entertained many political friends at Langford Court. In 1803 the country feared that Napoleon was planning to invade England. Addington became colonel of the East Battalion of the Mendip Legion of Cavalry. This comprised 70 men from local villages who had been quickly recruited and trained to fight. Addington presented them with the King's Colour and the Regiment Colour but the troop was not needed and the Colours were hung at Langford Court, only to be eaten by moths. They were moved to Burrington Church in 1904.

John Hiley Addington died in 1818 and Langford Court was passed on to his son Haviland Addington. The information from the census returns shows that in 1841 Haviland Addington, age 50 and of independent means, was living at Langford Court with his sister Mary. In 1851 and 1861 he is recorded as still living there with his sister and four servants. His occupation is shown to be a magistrate.

Haviland Addington died in 1869 and the house was inherited by his brother Henry Unwin Addington. He was a civil servant in the Foreign Office and had negotiated a treaty for the suppression of the slave trade. He was thought to be 'irredeemably stupid' and was nicknamed 'Pumpy' in the Foreign Office. He lived at Langford Court for a year before he died and his widow sold Langford Court to Colonel Llewellyn in 1870.

Col. Llewellyn
1847-1914

Colonel Llewellyn came from South Wales and had been involved in coal mining. He had just married Mary Blanche Somers of Mendip Lodge in 1869, prior to moving to Langford Court. His wife was the great, great granddaughter of John Jones, formerly of Langford Court. Colonel Llewellyn was well respected and beloved throughout the county. He was an M.P. a deputy lieutenant, a county councillor and a magistrate. In 1900 he was re-elected as an M.P. despite being absent on active service in the war in South Africa.

Blanche Llewellyn died in 1906 and Colonel Llewellyn moved to Langford Court Farm. Langford Court was rented by Mrs Richardson and her step-daughter. Mrs Richardson and her sister had been adopted by William Henry Wills and his wife, Elizabeth, when their parents died. They were Elizabeth's nieces. William Henry became the 1st Lord Winterstoke and Chairman of the Imperial Tobacco Company. The Winterstokes spent a lot of time at the Coombe Lodge Estate, Blagdon, which was their country seat.

Colonel Llewellyn was also a director of the Great Western Railway and he instigated the Wrington Vale Light Railway. This line opened in December 1901 and ran from Congresbury to Blagdon via Wrington, Langford and Burrington. Colonel Llewellyn used his influence to provide a station at Langford, half a mile from the village centre. He was able to walk across a field and the train would stop for him to board.

Colonel Llewellyn died in Devon in 1914. His body was brought back from Devon on a special train for his burial at Burrington.

The Collegiate School, Langford Court, near Bristol

In 1917, Langford House was bought by Sir George Wills, Bt. and in 1919 it was occupied by his son, George Vernon Wills. Sir George, whose father was Lord Winterstoke's first cousin, had inherited Coombe Lodge in 1911. After his death in 1928, his son, now Sir Vernon Wills, commissioned Sir George Oatley to build a new house to replace Coombe Lodge but, in 1931, before it was completed, he died at Langford Court. Sometime after this his widow, Lady Jean Wills and her family, Mary, Peter and John, moved to Coombe Lodge. Miss Vera Wills, Sir Vernon's sister, lived at Langford Court until she died in 1939. Sir Peter Wills was killed in action in Italy in the Second World War and his younger brother, John inherited the title.

For a short while Langford Court was used as a school. The Collegiate School from Winterbourne in Bristol moved out of the war-torn city in June 1940 and stayed at Langford Court until December 1945.

The remainder of the lease was given to Miss Hilda Wills of Horton Court. She was also a sister of Sir Vernon and wanted to be near her family but unfortunately she died just a few months after moving in.

Westwing School moved into Langford Court in December 1946, from its wartime refuge at Boskenwyn, near Penzance. This was a girls', privately owned, independent school whose name was derived from its very first premises in the west wing of a house at Ryde on the Isle of Wight. It was run by Professor and Mrs Alicia Barker (headmistress) with the help of her step-daughter, Shirley, and Miss Young. On Sunday mornings during term time a crocodile of forty to fifty girls could be seen walking up the road to the footpath at the top of Langford Lane and across the fields to Burrington Church for the morning service. Westwing School remained at Langford Court until September 1960.

Sir John Wills and his family, Lady Jane, David, Anthony, Rupert and Julian moved back into Langford Court in 1961. Sir John had been born at Langford Court in 1928 and became the Lord Lieutenant of Avon. He died in 1998 and after his death, the house passed to his son Sir David Wills.

The house was originally built in an 'E' shape which was the fashion for country houses in Elizabethan times.

In Whalley's time Langford Court had a large, wainscoted hall with a splendid Adam mantelpiece which was changed to a carved stone one when he took the original to Mendip Lodge. To the left of the hall was a panelled morning room and to the right was a dining room with a magnificent ceiling. A beautiful drawing room with a finely moulded cornice was on the south side of the dining room. There was an ante-room off this drawing room and another off the morning room and together they formed the ends of the letter 'E'.

There is an old window within a glass porch which was an alms window through which meat, drink or money was handed to the many travellers trudging the Bristol to

Exeter highway. It is now in a broom cupboard which was originally an outside wall of the kitchen. It is still sometimes referred to as 'the tramps' window'.

A tablet with a Latin inscription was found under the floor in a loft of an outbuilding. It might have stood over the lintel of the old house or Whalley may have brought it back from his continental travels to use at Mendip Lodge. It says:

> *Christus meus et omnia*
> *Christe casas intra mecum*
> *Donec coelos intrem tecum*
>
> *Ano Dom 1651*

Translated this reads:

> *Christ enter thou my house*
> *And be with me until I enter Heaven*
> *With Thee.*
>
> *The year of our Lord 1651*

The date of 1651 is verified by that above the fan light.

An extra wing was added to Langford Court, in 1875, which provided even more space for entertaining.

Col. Llewellyn gave a Christmas ball in 1886 and issued 400 invitations. A temporary adaptation to the house provided a ballroom adjoining the drawing room. It was constructed in such a way that both rooms could be used for dancing. By removing the casements of a window, a bay was made to provide a platform for the quadrille band. The floor was overlaid with dancing cloth. The rooms were draped with pale blue cloth caught up with bouquets of primroses. The twenty-four foot high ceiling was draped and festooned with cream-coloured cloth overlaid with a network of fine cord. The illumination was provided by two cut glass chandeliers each bearing one hundred candles. Two ten-foot high oval mirrors were put in the ballroom to reflect the dancers. Several engraved Venetian glasses were mounted on velvet and sparkled in the candlelight. The ballroom was heated by two fires which were tended from the outside and protected by brass lattice fronts.

In Langford Court's early days the front elevation would have been the north-facing side. This was changed at some stage and the south-facing side became the front. This change may account for the fact there is no grand staircase which would be a typical feature of this type of country house.

A house such as Langford Court may well have a ghost. In the 1930s two servants were asked by Lady Jean Wills why they had been cleaning upstairs. The two ladies replied that they had not been upstairs at all. But Lady Jean had distinctly heard footsteps…...!

Postcard of Langford Court
(See Colour Plate 38, Page 130)

-2-

Langford Place

Jenny Hooper

A Grade II Georgian house with a natural grey render, today, Langford Place is composed of three named homes - Clifton House, Yew Trees and Langford Place. The whole building stands in one and a half acres. The house is said to date back to 1823 although land tax records first show an owner/occupier in 1826.

Langford Place has been the name of a house on this site long before the dwelling built in the 1820s. Somerset Record Office has a map with a house on the same site in 1771. Apart from the cellars, there is no real evidence of the earlier building. Today, the present building is a fine example of an elegant Georgian country house.

The first person to own the present house was Samuel Capper from 1826 until 1838. He was paying land tax of 16 s. 3/4d. for the house, gardens and stables, and 4s. 4d. for John Richardson's home. John Richardson lived in the gardener's cottage where the two semi detached houses called Langford Place Gardens are situated today. The size of the whole building in 1838 was very much as it is today, but with the addition of Yew Trees' present drawing room, as shown on the 1998 map.

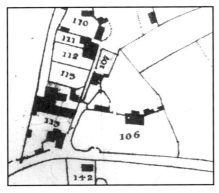

1838 Tithe Map

1998 Map

Samuel Capper does not appear in the 1841 census, and it is possible that Henry Collings, a gentleman of independent means, was living at Langford Place with his family at this time. By 1851, Mary Somers is believed to have been occupying the house; was this the start of the long ownership of Langford Place by the Somers family?

Kelly's Directory shows a De Merle Esq. at Langford Place in 1872.

The house was acquired by Benjamin Edward Somers aged 24 years in 1875, and it was the Somers family who added much of the extra land and dwellings to the Langford Place Estate. The land stretched either side of Saxon Street and reached as far as the River Yeo.

The house was very much alive and part of the community for the next 80 years. There was a butler, cook, lady's maid, housekeeper and many servants employed to keep the house running smoothly. The 1881 census shows Elizabeth Somers aged 63 years as head of the household, living with her 21 year old nephew. According to Kelly's Directory, The Hon. Lincoln Edwin Stanhope was in residence at Langford Place in 1889 and he also had a home in Princess Gate, Knightsbridge, London.

Research has shown that a Miss Burgess was the head of the household in 1902, living with her cousins, Miss Annie Christie aged 42 and Miss Mary Connor aged 50. The three ladies were related to the owners of Langford Court, and for this reason Langford Place became known for some years as the Dower House.

Benjamin Edward Somers MA JP returned to live at Langford Place from 1910 to 1919. In the 1913 Enclosure Act, Benjamin Somers also owned The Old Post Office and Lodge Farm. Somers sold both Langford Place Farm and Langford Place in 1919 by auction. The farmhouse was described as *"an attractive thatched farmhouse"*, situated between yew trees on the side of the present A38. These were on the site of the Kingfisher Green estate which used to be called Yew Trees. Langford Place was described as *"a very attractive country residence occupying a charming and well enclosed position within five minutes walk of Langford Station. Almost in the centre of the village, and having an extensive frontage to the main road with stabling, motor or coach houses, gardener's cottage, tennis and other lawns, kitchen gardens, first class orchard etc. The residence, which is approached by a carriage drive (Saxon Street), is in excellent decorative repair throughout."*

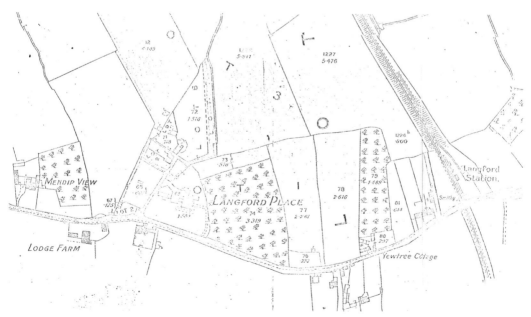

1919 map of Langford Place, farm & lands to be sold by auction

Phillip Twills Marshall bought Langford Place in 1923, having lived at Hylsbroke (also in Lower Langford) since 1914. Phillip Marshall spent much of his time during the week in London, being a member of the Marshall family of Marshall and Snelgrove - the large London department store which survived until 1969. Phillipa Marshall, his daughter, lived on in the area for a further 30 years. During this period the large kitchen garden was looked after by Mr Kitchen who lived in The Old Post Office. The remaining parts of the garden were looked after by a gardener who lived in the gardener's cottage at the bottom of Saxon Street. I have been told there were six full time gardeners and eight servants working at Langford Place during this time. We had a visit from an elderly lady who had worked in the house as a maid. She said some of the staff lived in the house and some out; some were full time and some part time. It even had a bakery, and a baker came to make bread and cakes three times a week!

The Marshalls sold Langford Place in 1947 to William Henry Beale, from Stoke Bishop in Bristol, for £6,000. The University of Bristol bought Langford Place in 1949 for £13,500 to use as a home for the Clinical Director of Veterinary Medicine. Professor Ewer and his family lived happily in the house in the late 1950s. However, using the house for one family became too expensive for the University and they converted the house into three flats. Fortunately they did not damage too much of the original fabric.

During this period the Hills, Laings, McCreas and Wilsons lived in the house to name but a few. During the University's ownership the kitchen garden was sold and all the outlying lands of Langford Place. The orchard and tennis court were developed and a new house was built in the 1960s, named The Old Garden. At much the same time, the stables were sold and converted into a house, now called The Stables. The gardener's cottage at the bottom of Saxon Street was pulled down and two houses were built. (Langford Place Gardens). In 1977, Langford Place, in a sorry state, due to general neglect complete with a fox living in the house, was sold at auction for £24,500. Mr Edward Callaghan and Mr. Martin Sessions Hodge purchased it and developed the building into three homes.

There were threats to demolish the whole property in 1976. A petition in the village strongly objected to the plan and the house was saved – thank goodness!

-3-

The Old Post Office

Juliet Fowles

This cottage which was once sited close to one of the Langford tanneries, has served as a family home, a shop and a post office for more than 150 years. It would have had a central role in the life of the village throughout that period.

The cottage, now called the Old Post Office, sits on the corner of Saxon Street and Langford Road. I am not sure when the house was built but it is clearly marked on a map dated 1762. It was once two "one-up, one-down" homes which were owned in 1838 by Thomas Brookman. He also owned the tannery which was alongside the cottage. The cottage attracted an annual tithe of 3s 5½ d. One occupant was Thomas Thorn, who is described in the 1841 census return as a shopkeeper of 50. He lived there with his wife, Sarah (40), and their two sons, Thomas aged 3 and John aged 1. The other occupant was Maria Pool, who had an eleven-year-old servant, Louisa Bath.

By the time of the 1851 census, Thomas, whose surname is now spelt Thorne, was a widower and his age is given as 64. He was living with his two youngest children, Joseph aged 8 and Fanny aged 7, who had both been born in this parish of Burrington. His occupation is given as agricultural labourer. It is Ann Parker who is described as "Post Office keeper" in the 1851 census return. She is aged 41 and lives with her husband, John, a master carpenter of 43 and their three children, Sarah Ann (14), John Henry (9) and Thomas (2). They had been neighbours of Thomas Thorn ten years earlier. I wonder if the shop had really been run by Sarah Thorn and the business was taken over by Ann Parker when Sarah died.

By 1861, Ann Parker had been widowed and was described in the census as "Grocer and postmistress". She was living with her son, Thomas (13). On census night, Thomas Thorne, now 74, was staying nearby with a family called Adams.

A different member of the Parker family is recorded as living at the Old Post Office in all the census returns from 1871 to 1901. This is John Parker, who was born in Blackmoor in 1835, the son of Thomas and Sarah Parker. Like his father and also his predecessor at the Post Office, John was a carpenter. According to the census returns of 1871 and 1881, he was married to Ann, who was born in Bitton in 1833. In 1871, the house is called "Grocers Shop" and the Post Office had moved to different premises. In 1881, Ann's occupation is described as "shopkeeper". A post office is not mentioned in this census return but the 1883 Ordnance Survey map names the Parker's cottage as "Post Office". It also shows that the tannery yard had gone by then.

In the 1891 and 1901 census returns, the house is called "Post Office" and John is described as "Carpenter and postmaster". A busy man! He is now married to Anne, who was born near Leominster in Herefordshire in 1843. They have John's unmarried younger sister, Sarah, who is the same age as Anne, living with them. In 1891, a nephew, Thomas Roberts, was also there and employed as a post office assistant. The Burrington and Havyatt Enclosure Act confirms that John Parker still occupied The Old Post Office in 1913 and shows that the property was owned by Benjamin Somers of Mendip Lodge. He also owned Langford Place.

The post office ran up until the 1914/18 war. Being on the main postal road, I expect it was busy. It closed and, sadly, the house became derelict and remained empty for some

*The original oak front door of The Old Post Office - a 17th century strap and hinge door
(See Colour Plate 3, Page 113)*

years. The 5th May 1952 saw the property bought by the University of Bristol from Percy and Winifred Quick, as part of its expansion plans in the village. It was renamed The Old Post Office. The house was renovated but still retains the beamed ceilings, tongue and groove doors and the original oak front door. The loft space was converted to make a much needed third bedroom.

On the 28th May 1970, the house changed hands again and was bought from the University by Margaret Maud Hind and her husband for £3,950. They erected a carport and antique showroom. In 1971, they doubled the height of the wall alongside the road. Was the traffic getting too bad then?

Michael and Ann Bailey briefly owned the house and bought the adjoining land from the University of Bristol and put it to orchard. They converted the showroom to an annex.

1997 saw the present owners, the Fowles family move into the house. They were longstanding residents of the village, having previously lived at Somerlea. A conservatory was added, as the one room downstairs is crowded for the family today. We can't imagine what it was like when the Brookmans and Thorns lived here. And that was before the kitchen extension was added in Victorian times!

-4-

Laurel Cottage

Stefan Marjoram

Laurel Cottage is one of several simple farm labourers' houses in Saxon Street. It was perhaps built in about 1800, though it is very hard to attach an exact date. Originally a two-up, two-down with a lean-to washroom at the rear, a two-story extension was added to one end in about 1910. It was only in 1973 that the lean-to containing its well and water pump was extended and modernised.

When we started research on the previous occupiers of Laurel Cottage, we found that very little was known about who lived here, save that the Tithe map of 1838 shows a Mr Thomas Dyer and family. The same names appear in the 1841 and subsequent census returns. Tantalisingly, several copperplate names have been found written on the plaster next to the front entrance but again, these cannot be matched to any in the census returns.

However, in May 2008, we were contacted by a Terry Dyer from Eastbourne who had seen the Langford History Group website, and had subsequently emailed us concerning his ancestors, William Dyer and his wife, Jane. He wondered whether the Dyers that we had described in the first edition of this book might be related.

A visit was arranged, and we discovered that Terry's ancestor William Dyer had in fact lived at our neighbour's cottage, Iona. Thomas Dyer, a relation to William had occupied Laurel Cottage, with his wife, Ann.

It was her family whose signatures, dating from the early 1800s, were adorned on our wall, hence the absence of the name Dyer!

Remains of original thatched roof showing elm rafters

The current owners are renovating the property using traditional materials. This includes the complete removal of modern cement render, which has been replaced with lime *(See Colour Plate 5, Page 114)*.

The work has revealed several interesting features. The roof space contains the remains of an earlier thatched roof. The ceilings and stud walls use reeds instead of laths, and elm has been used for the original roof timbers and upper floors. Sadly the floor boards were too badly damaged by insect attack to be salvaged.

Remains of original thatched roof showing elm rafters and the interior of a reed and plaster stud wall.

The garden has also yielded some interesting finds including ox skulls (perhaps from the Saxon Street tannery?), a Roman coin from the time of Trajan, a fake (copper) half crown and a copper Trade Token – issued in 1812, when there was a shortage of small denomination coinage.

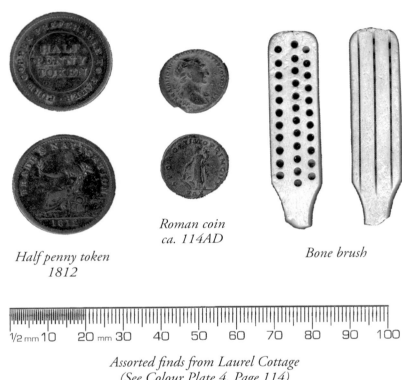

Half penny token
1812

Roman coin
ca. 114AD

Bone brush

½ mm 10   20 mm 30   40   50   60   70   80   90   100

Assorted finds from Laurel Cottage
(See Colour Plate 4, Page 114)

Finally, when lifting the boards, we found what looked to be the remains of an old leather shoe. These were sometimes placed in chimneys or near doorways and windows to ward off evil – it seems to be working so far!

-5-

Lodge Farm

Michael Norman

Lodge Farm is listed Grade II as "a possible 17th century core with early 19th century addition". The house is located on the south side of the old toll road, at the eastern end of the village. It has a double-gabled roof, and the timbers in the southern section have been dated to about 1800, though it is possible that this roof replaced an earlier structure. The principal walls are built of stone and are 50cm (20in) or more thick. Some of the sash windows at the eastern and western ends of the house are in the gothic revival style, but in general relatively few original features have survived. The associated barn and walled garden have probably been in existence since at least 1838, when they appeared on the tithe map.

James Kingcott (farmer with about 4 acres), who is listed as 'Owner and Occupier' of Lodge Farm in the 1838 Burrington tithe apportionment, had married Elizabeth Haskins at St. Mary Redcliffe in 1835. At the time of their marriage, Elizabeth Haskins was a widow with three children. At the age of seventeen, she had married Henry Haskins (a widower of seventy-eight) in Burrington. In the 1841 census, the family is listed as living in Devonshire House, Blackmoor, and in the 1842 Churchill tithe apportionments, James is listed as occupier of Devonshire house (the owner being Joseph Wood). By 1848 the family appears to have moved back into Burrington parish, but it is not certain whether or not they had returned to Lodge Farm. James and Elizabeth had nine children, and in 1857 the family took an assisted passage to Australia where James established a Greengrocer's shop in Sydney[1].

The cruel fate of James Kingcott's cousins, John and James Rowley, is a reminder of how callous society could be[2]. Accused of setting fire to wheat mows in the village of Kenn, they were sentenced to death. James was later reprieved and transported, but died before reaching Australia. John and two other men were executed in September 1830 at the scene of the crime (the last such execution to take place in England). The men were transported in a cart, each man sitting on his coffin, from Ilchester jail together with their executioner and his assistants. Accompanied by various dignitaries, including the Chief Constable and the High Sheriff, as well as one hundred special constables, the cavalcade took over six hours to reach Kenn. An estimated fifteen to twenty thousand spectators witnessed the execution.

According to Kelly's Directory, in 1872 Edward Gallop (who later moved to 'Mendip View') and his family were living in Lodge Farm, but by 1891 Annie Chapman (widow of forty seven years, Registrar of Births and Deaths) occupied the house with her children Kate, Abraham, Ethel and Emmeline (the enumerator for the Burrington census of 1901 was Emmeline Chapman). In 1914, Abraham Slade Chapman (farmer) was listed as Deputy Registrar of Births and Deaths. According to the Enclosure Act of 1913, the owner at that time was Benjamin Somers of Langford Place. Later, Lodge Farm became part of the Wills Estate. Mr Morris remembers that in the early 1930s he would go with a jug to the dairy (now a kitchen) at the back of the house to buy cream. A Miss Chapman still lived in the house until around the end of the Second World War. In the 1950s the house was divided into two dwellings and the northern section of gabled roof removed to create a flat roof.

[1] *"Kingcott Place – The family from Somerset", Loris Kingcott. Hippo Books, 2002*

[2] *"The Kenn Hangings of 1830: the full story" Lilly, D and J; Clevedon, 1993*

Aerial photograph (1964)

Mr and Mrs Illingworth, who were succeeded by Mr Roberts and family, occupied the rear part of the house. The front was occupied at first by Mr and Mrs Callow, and in 1957 Reg Williams, who had been employed as a gardener on the Wills estate before the war, moved in with his wife Bertha and two younger daughters. Gena Williams, who was three years old at the time the family moved into the house, lived there until 1993.

In 1993, Julian and Fiona Wills purchased the house from the Wills Estate and carried out extensive renovations, converting it back into a single-occupancy dwelling. Lodge Farm is now owned and occupied by Debbie and Michael Norman, who purchased the property in 2004.

-6-

Nash House

Jane Dixon

The present owners of Nash House, the decoration of which is contemporary with that of an early seventeenth century 'upper class gentleman's residence' would like to think that it was one of the more 'respectable' residences referred to by Rutter in his History of Somerset of 1829. The house was built on the south side of the Turnpike Road that ran between Bristol and Exeter. The house's proximity to this road would have influenced both the appearance and fortunes of the building and its outbuildings.

Nash House is thought to be the oldest surviving property in the village of Lower Langford but had no official name until 1831 when the first reference is made to Nashes. I refer to it as Nash House throughout the following chapter, apart from when it was known as Laburnum House in the years between 1840 and 1945. It is an impressive three storey house that would seem to be of Jacobean origin. When the house was built it must have been one of the few substantial houses in the parish. It is built of rose coloured limestone or sandstone and would have had a thatched roof. The outside is now rendered and the roof is pantiled. The house has mullioned windows and there are stone drip moulds over the windows on the north, east and west sides. There are five windows which have been blocked up (one was unblocked in 1983). These mullioned windows are compatible with early seventeenth century design. The main doors are most likely to be the original doors of the house and their frames are of the same period. Inside the house the original finely decorated beams can be seen, and there is evidence which shows how lath and reed partitions might have divided the space. There are traces of earlier staircases, blocked up fireplaces in the attic, roof timbers which do not correspond with the shape of the present roof and dressed flagstone floors downstairs.

Beam end

Door frame

The plans suggest that the first Nash House may have been a rectangular dwelling with two symmetrical wings on the north side with an open court between them making the traditional E shape that is associated with the Jacobean style. It is also possible that the attics had dormer windows facing north. New windows may have been put into the east and west ends of the old structure to match the windows on the north side. Two of these windows still have their bars and there is evidence that the other windows, both downstairs and upstairs on the front of the house had barred windows. These alterations must have been finished before 1696 when the window tax was first introduced as all five of the end windows have been blocked up. The open court on the north front of the house has also been incorporated into the house bringing the front door into line with the front of the two wings providing an entrance hall and a new staircase. We know this was done before 1914 because of evidence provided by old photographs. Perhaps at this time the roof was altered to being the double roof running from east to west as at present, from having been one east west roof and two north south roofs. Between 1818 and 1842 an extension of one large room downstairs with a connecting staircase to a room upstairs, was built onto the west side of the house. In 1983 this extension was incorporated into the main house and the slope of the roof on the north side altered as part of extensive renovations.

The following summary of the history of Nash House is taken from our own deeds dating back to 1814. We have no record of when the house was built or its history prior to 1735. Information has been taken from the Turnpike Map (1818), The Tithe Maps, information from The Somerset Records Office in Taunton and the library in Weston-super-Mare and a booklet on Burrington Church and Village by Christopher Marsden-Smedley. Old documents are difficult to read and understand but I hope this is a fair account of the history of Nash House. There are a large number of leases, releases, indentures and documents referring to Nash House but the people who lived and died in Nash House are rarely mentioned. It is only after the 1841 census that a picture begins to emerge about those people and how they may have lived.

Until 1825 Nash House was part of the Manor of Langford in the parish of Burrington in the county of Somerset. There may be earlier documents about the house in the records of Langford Court which in the eighteenth century was the seat of the Jones Family who were both wealthy and influential and are buried at Burrington. The earliest mention of the property is in 1738 when there is reference to a lease and release, not a sale, made between Edward Jones of Langford Court and George and Thomas Musgrave, Mary Musgrave his wife and their daughter Mary. (Edward Jones married a Mary Musgrave and their daughter Elizabeth was born in 1740. How interesting it would be if the daughter of Nash House had married the boy next door, Edward Jones of Langford Court, but I have not been able to confirm this.)

Edward Jones died in 1743 and his lands and estate passed to his daughter Elizabeth (1740-1801) who later married John Withers Sherwood of Sidcot. In 1762 an indenture was drawn up between J Withers Sherwood, Elizabeth Sherwood, John Adderley and Robert Jefferies and Richard Jenkyns. John Sherwood died in 1770.

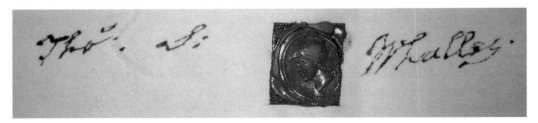

Signature of Thomas S. Whalley
(See Colour Plate 6, Page 115)

In 1773 The Revd. Thomas Sedgwick Whalley makes his first appearance in the deeds of Nash House. He must have been engaged to Elizabeth Sherwood at this time as there is a record of a lease and release between Elizabeth Sherwood, Thomas Whalley and Sir James Langham and Richard Jenkyns. Their marriage took place on 6 January 1774 at St. Marylebone in Middlesex. In 1780 there is record of a lease and release between T. S. Whalley and wife and Robert Tricker. Between 1782 and 1788 there are references to The Revd. Whalley and his wife being defendants in a court hearing involving Nash House. We do not know what these proceedings were about. Elizabeth Whalley died in 1801 and after her death her remaining properties became the property of her husband.

In 1814 'all that messuage, tenement or dwelling house with the garden or orchard thereunto belonging containing by admeasurement two roods and two perches (more or less) bounded on the north by the turnpike road leading to Bristol and formerly in the occupation of Simon Smeathes but since of Ann Smeathes and also one close of meadow or pasture ground a small part thereof an orchard containing by admeasurements four acres, one rood and nineteen perches (more or less) and bounded on the south by the said turnpike road and also all that close of arable ground containing by admeasurement three acres or thereabouts and adjoined the last mentioned close of ground and also all that close of meadow or pasture ground containing by admeasurement six acres, two roods and twenty eight perches (more or less) adjoining the first mentioned close on the south all which said messuage and several closes or pieces of arable meadow and pasture ground are therein expressed to be situate lying and being at Lower Langford and to be part or reputed part of the manor Langford in the County of Somerset.' Put into simple English, this says that the house and some fourteen acres of land were leased as a single unit. Seven and a half acres on the north side of the turnpike road and about six and half acres on the south side of the turnpike road.

Before Elizabeth Whalley died she and her husband had been living abroad and he disposed of Langford Court to the Addington Family but must have kept some land and properties within the parish. In the years between 1804 and 1814 the lease of Nash House was held by Dr.. Whalley (he had become a Doctor of Divinity in 1803) and Richard Jenkyns and Jno. Hiley Addington and Hiley Addington (the new owners of Langford Court). In 1814 it was redrawn between Revd. Frixham Whitter and T. S. Whalley and John Whitley

Towards the end of 1814 a lease was drawn up between Dr.. Whalley, George Fear and George Pope. George Fear, a schoolteacher from Harptree, however had undischarged debts and the trustees of the lease were unable to find a buyer for the remainder of the lease. Dr. Whalley agreed to buy the lease back for five shillings and a peppercorn.

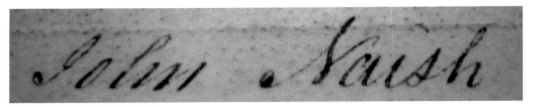

Signature of John Naish

In 1818 a lease and release is drawn up between Dr. Whalley and John Naish a 'gentleman' of Churchill. This lease was renewed on an annual basis until 1825 when the property was purchased outright by John Naish. A quotation from a letter dated July 10th 1819 from Dr.. Whalley to his nephew refers to 'Mr. Naish my faithful old bailiff and zealous friend'. It is I think a reasonable assumption to make that John Naish, and Mr. Naish were the same person. The bailiff, an influential and respected person, would be in a good position to purchase lands and houses in Langford from a financially embarrassed Dr. Whalley and later censuses show the Naish Family as owning fields and properties in the village.

John Naish died on 11th July 1826 and after numerous bequests to his nephews and nieces had been met and his widow provided for, his remaining assets and properties became the property of his brother Abraham Naish who was not referred to as a 'gentleman' but as a 'grocer' from Hampshire, and his wife Sarah (see Chapter 11).

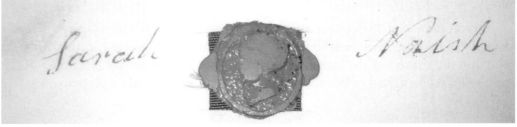

Signatures of Abraham Naish and Sarah Naish
(See Colour Plate 7, Page 115)

Land Tax records referring to Nash House show that in 1832 and subsequent years the amount payable on the house and garden was seven shillings and ten pence farthing. The fields referred to as Cox's and Dyer's and in the ownership of Dr. Whalley, John Naish, Abraham Naish and Benjamin Somers had a tax levied on them, the sum of one pound and seven shillings being payable on Cox's. This is recorded in the records from 1811 onwards. Between 1829 and 1837 the deeds state the house was lived in by a William Badman.

In 1831 an indenture was drawn up between Abraham Naish, his wife Sarah and Benjamin Somers. Nash House, its outbuildings, about ten acres of land and mineral rights as well as grazing rights on the common and any rights to waste land in the parish was to be leased to Dr.. Benjamin Somers, a Doctor of Medicine, who lived at No 12 Woburn Square in the county of Middlesex. The fee for all this was to be one peppercorn and five shillings. I can only assume that this is a presale document as the Conveyance of the property took place in 1831 and for £355 Nash House was sold to Dr.. Somers.

Signatures of Benjamin Somers
(See Colour Plate 8, Page 115)

In 1837 a document drawn up by Thomas Somers Barrister at Law, of Lincoln's Inn Chambers and son of Benjamin Somers begins:

'*Know all Men......All that mesuage or tenement with outhouses garden orchard arable and pasture land thereto belonging called Cox's containing together be estimation ten acres (more or less) situate at Lower Langford aforesaid with appurtements except a certain right or certain rights of common of pasture and with commonable rights to the said mesuage or dwelling house belonging or appertaining in order and upon certain commons and commonable or waste lands situate within the said parish of Burrington or elsewhere in the county of Somerset*'.

It goes on to suggest that some ten acres of land belonging to Nash House was sold to Richard Burges. He was a plasterer and tiler who met his third wife Sarah in Langford while she was waiting to meet the coach. Richard Burges was building or rebuilding his own house at the time which was Dring Cottage (see Chapter 8).

Richard Burges may have lived in Nash House after he bought the property but the 1842 Tithe Apportionment and the 1841 census show Richard Burges owning three properties in Lower Langford, No. 135a Laburnum House, now known as Nash House and lived in by Bevis Thiery. (The 1841 census also shows Bevis Thiery as living at Charterhouse Ville, his age is approximately 65 and he farmed approximately 460 acres and employed six labourers in Somerset.) No. 136, now known as Dring Cottage and lived in by Richard Burges, his wife Sarah and six children, and No. 137 Rose Cottage, which must have been two very small cottages and lived in by Robert and Elizabeth Vicary, and James and Maria Hollier and their two children Elizabeth and George. Robert Vicary and James Hollier were both agricultural labourers.

Richard Burges died in 1853 leaving his widow Sarah and unmarried children in Dring Cottage. In his will it states that James Stallard, a schoolteacher, was the occupant of Laburnum House. The stables and carthouse were occupied by Henry Baber whom a later census in 1881 shows as being a shoemaker.

The same census also shows Sarah Burges a widow and her unmarried daughter living in Dring Cottage running a grocer's shop. Next door to them are Mr. and Mrs. Jones bootmakers this could be Rose Cottage, and next door to them is a boarding school, run by Henry and Eliza Northover. He is 31, she 28. They have three children of their own and fourteen scholars aged between eight and fourteen. There is also a 20 year old general servant by the name of Emma Norley. It is not known whether this boarding school was based in Nash House, or Milfort, but the WI book produced in 1975 makes reference to Nash House as having been a school. It is hard to believe that Nash House could have been a boarding school but there are six rooms on the ground floor four with fireplaces, six rooms on the first floor with at least three fireplaces and five proper rooms on the second floor, two of which have had fireplaces in them. This same school later moved to Sutledge House at the other end of the village, a house which is smaller than Nash House.

If Nash House ever was a school, it had closed down by the time of the 1871 census. Widow Burges and her daughter Sarah Sabina were living in Dring cottage. Next door to them were two empty properties (Rose Cottages?) and then next door to them most likely in Nash House lived Edwin and Eliza Migley and their three children, Edwin, Alice and George. Edwin Migley worked as a carpenter and joiner.

In the 1881 census Henry Baber who was occupying the stables and carthouse is shown as living in Langford. He is forty five years old and a bootmaker and insurance agent. His wife Sarah is also forty five, his son George is twenty two and works as a gardener and domestic servant. He has two daughters Ellen and Jane aged fourteen and ten who are still at school. Unfortunately the census does not make it clear where they were living and it may be that he only did his work as a bootmaker in the outbuildings at Nash House. The 1881 census has a family called Durston living next door to Mrs. Burges and her daughter. They had six children Mr. Durston and his eldest son worked as bootmakers. There were five younger children still at school.

Sarah Burges died on 28 October 1884 and was buried at Burrington. The three properties that now seem to be known collectively as Burgesville were left to her children. Their unmarried daughter Sarah Sabina who was still living in Dring Cottage, sold Laburnum House and its outbuildings, (probably including Rose Cottage) to George Young on 18th May 1897. A large part of the documents relating to this sale are making sure that no window was ever to be put in the connecting walls between Laburnum House and Dring Cottage.

The 1891 census shows George Young, his wife Izett and three sons already living in a house next door but one to Sarah Sabina Burges. George Young is described as a forty six year old commons (foodstuffs) carrier. In the field behind Nash House is a cart dip which is a paved track to allow carts to be left in water overnight to stop the wheels warping. George Young presumably bought the house he was renting. He died on 12th February 1900 and left his estate to his wife Izett. Izett Young died in 1927 and Laburnum House was left to her son Charles. By the time of his death George Young had extended his business interests to being not only a carrier, but also a proprietor of horses and conveyances for letting or hire. It is not known whether his widow Izett stayed on in Laburnum House till her death or not.

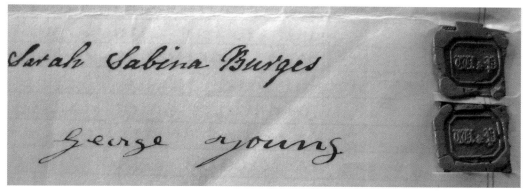

Signatures of Sarah Sabina Burges and George Young
(See Colour Plate 9, Page 115)

It is however known that the Browning Family were living in Laburnum House before the two World Wars. They would have been tenants of the Young Family and may have remained there until about 1945. William Henry Browning and his wife had four children. Their eldest son Edwin was killed in the First World War and his name is recorded in Burrington Church. Their other son became a grocer and had a business in Churchill. One of their daughters married and went to live in Yatton and their youngest daughter married her next door neighbour Mr. Harris from Hylsbrook House.

William Henry Browning was a joiner and carpenter and was also the village undertaker. All his businesses were conducted from Laburnum House and its outbuildings. The 1931 map shows that two substantial buildings had been constructed in the garden and orchard neither of which exist now. They may have been built to stable the horses of George Young or to build coffins for Mr. Browning.

The Browning Family

After the death of Izett Young in 1927 until 1945, the ownership of Laburnum House was passed between members of the Young Family. They were now based in Weston-super-Mare and were running a taxi business. The house appears to have been mortgaged and remortgaged on a number of occasions and was eventually put up for auction on 8th November 1945. The auction took place at Laburnum House and it was bought by Mr. Victor Cross of Richmond House, Langford for £2,000. The property was now reduced in size to 1 Acre, 2 Roods and 30 Perches.

Signature of Victor Cross

Victor Cross's purchase proved to be a shrewd investment. Four years later after modernisation Laburnum House, now renamed Nash House was sold to Alice Geraldine Overton Faunthorpe a widow from Guildford for £7,250.

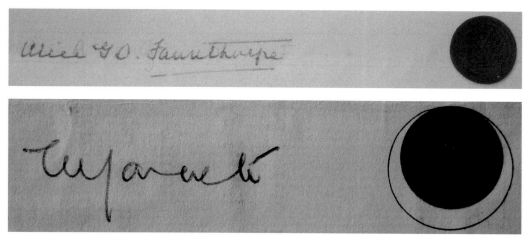

Signatures of Alice G. O. Faunthorpe and T. W. Garnett

Nash House changed hands again in 1952 for £7,500 when Mrs. Faunthorpe sold the property to Mr. T. W. Garnett a stockbroker, who was living in Blagdon. Mr. and Mrs. Garnett continued to live in the house until the death of Mr. Garnett in 1983. By that time the house had become the property of Avon Executor and Trustee Company.

In 1983 Nash House, now a Grade II listed property, was sold to John Dixon, an orthopaedic surgeon and his wife Jane. They paid £90,000 for the house and its remaining land and spent a further £60,000 restoring the old house. The following is a list showing some of the work that had to be done and gives an idea of the state of the house at this time:-

The roofs were taken off, the old thatch or insulation was removed and the squirrels evicted.

The extension on the west end of the house was modernized and connected into the house on the first floor.

A tower of three fireplaces and their chimneys going the height of the house at the east end and installed after the blocking up of the windows was removed.

Ceilings collapsed and had to be replaced.

The rising damp which by now extended to the first floor had to be dealt with and all ground floor plaster was removed and replaced. All the floors on the ground floor were lifted and relaid with a damp course being installed.

Fireplaces were unblocked.

When the window on the east end was opened up the original Jacobean window frame was found to be still in place.

All the windows on the south side were redesigned and replaced. Drains, electricity and plumbing were all replaced and the house connected to the main drainage.

The third floor was reconnected to the main house by replacing a ladder with proper stairs and all the rooms in the attic were given new floors.

All the flagstones were lifted and relaid.

All this work was done under the competent supervision of the architect Christopher Marsden-Smedley who lives in Burrington and with the approval of the Conservation Officers from Weston super Mare. In November 1984 the Dixon family moved in and still live there.

Signatures of J. H. Dixon and Jane Dixon

-7-

Rose Cottage, Burgesville

Marilyn Orr

Rose Cottage dates back to the early seventeenth century with an early nineteenth century Victorian addition. A further addition was made in the late nineteenth century to the south gable.

There are three Rose Cottages in Langford, the other two being in Says Lane and on the A38. The deeds of 1890 describe Rose Cottage as being converted into two cottages at that time. In 1953, according to documentation, it was still described as two cottages but in 1954 it was described as one. There are no details as to its conversion. Some of the 19th century census returns show that there were two families living in the cottage or cottages. The Turnpike Map of 1818 shows only one cottage on the site. There may have been two families living there, as, to eke out a living, agricultural labourers did take in lodgers.

The cottage has a pantiled catslide roof and casement windows, apart from a small stair window between the washhouse and one of the outside walls of the cottage. It is constructed with wooden pegs rather than nails, with a flat chamfer inside and out and is unglazed, indicating early 17th century origins. The beams, front door and stair window are all compatible with an early 17th century building. The exterior walls are at least two feet thick. Although the external walls are now rendered, recent repairs to the rendering exposed the front wall and one of the chimneys as being built of rose coloured limestone, packed with hair, mortar, pins and snecks. One of the chimneys is built with terracotta Mendip stone, some twigs and lime mortar. The back garden houses a well, now filled in, and a pump next to the lean-to washhouse, now a bathroom. One of the residents of Rose Cottage, mentioned in the Census Returns, was a washerwoman. Not many cottages in the 17th century had a well or pump, which must have served the two cottages, so that the inhabitants did not have to walk down to the village pump for water. The washerwoman must have supplemented her income taking in washing and thanked her good fortune for having the necessary requisites to hand.

Dozens of old bottles, including poison bottles, have been dug up from the back garden, together with clay pipes, and ink wells which leads one to think that either an apothecary or a very ill person lived within at some time.

Apothecary bottles
(See Colour Plate 10, Page 116)

The cottage interior holds further clues as to its age. The rafters in the roof and one purlin show some smoke blackening. This may suggest that there was originally an open hall with an inserted ceiling and a 15th or 16th century building: if so, the hall would have been the main cooking and living area, open to the rafters, with a fire in the centre. This way of living was common in the 15th century. Towards the end of this period the practice developed of jettying an upper floor out into the hall, leaving only one bay (the smoke bay) open. It has been suggested by enthusiasts of vernacular architecture that the roof space was also lived in, as there are partitions still in place and original plasterwork over the remaining thatch.

Plasterwork in the roof

The roof comprises a central truss with two sets of chamfered purlins, a straight cut apex with a threaded ridge. In the passage downstairs there are the filled-in remains of near vertical stairs. At the beginning of the Victorian age a spiral staircase replaced the old one. The walls here are made of wattle and daub and the wooden stairs themselves, now carpeted, are crudely made with gaps between the woodwork.

Interior beams have cyma stops with deep chamfers and partitions. One of the beams bears markings where carpenters have seasoned and cut the wood (possibly elm) elsewhere, and carted it, in the form of a kit, to then be assembled in the cottage. The markings would indicate where the beams should be placed and interlocked. They were erected and secured with pegs and joints. The beams still bear the holes of the original partition of lath and reed that was woven between the staves and sealed with dabs of clay and dung and bound with hair and straw.

Fireplace
(See Colour Plate 11, Page 116)

Oven
(See Colour Plate 12, Page 117)

The present sitting room, which would have been the main living area, has a fireplace at each end, one being an inglenook with a blackened timber chamfered bressumer. This fireplace has a large oven and stairs around it. The second fireplace was inserted at a later date. There is also a spice cupboard next to the second fireplace. Some of the interior plank doors are put together with hand made nails. One door is only twenty inches wide: other doors have iron handgrips with a thumb latch lever at the top. The front door is made of planks and battens with strap hinges on pintels with spearheads, dating back to the early 17th century.

These features mentioned, together with the rounded corners and walls, are all poignant reminders of the evolution of the cottage from the early 17th century through to its early Victorian addition, such as the washhouse. In recent years the only major alterations have been a garage built in the 1970s and a single storey extension, built by previous owners in 1982/3, comprising ensuite bedroom, kitchen and dining room, which still has the remains of the framework of a very old door with pintels and spearheads. The extension has low ceilings and old roof pantiles in keeping with the cottage. The inglenook fireplace, which had been filled in, was rediscovered in the 1970s.

Rose Cottage is one of the most common names for a cottage. One fanciful theory as to why so many Rose Cottages exist is that many were made of rose coloured limestone, and not necessarily because of the roses that were grown in the garden

Before the late 19th or early 20th century growing vegetables would have been the priority rather than the more ornamental roses seen today.

In the 19th century there were shoemakers in every village. At one time there was a cordwainer living in this property who required dyes for his shoes made of Cordova Spanish leather. The dyes used then were made of rosaniline, a red or rose coloured dye. Rosaniline also provided the colour for pink wash rendering. The name rose colour could be a corruption of rosaniline.

In 1837 Nash House, previously known as Laburnum Cottage, and 10 acres of land, or garden as it was called in the 19th century, became the property of Richard Burges, a plasterer and tiler. This is also shown on the 1841 census. At that time Richard Burges lived with his wife Sarah and six children at site number 137 in the Tithe Apportionment Schedule. Rose Cottage was lived in by Robert & Elizabeth Vicary and James & Maria Hollier and their two children. Both men were agricultural labourers. The land comprising sites 135, 136 and 137 was known as Burgesville. A later census shows that the Holliers had another two children, the youngest being baby George, whilst living in Rose Cottage. Having two families (according to the 1841 & 1851 census returns), living in the cottage suggests that perhaps the current cottage was once two semi-detached cottages. The tithe map shows only one dwelling at 135.

The Hollier family seems to have been quite extensive in Lower Langford. The census returns in the 19th century show several households under the name of Hollier; apart from the young family in Rose Cottage, there appeared to be a James Hollier, a carrier, and Caroline Hollier a housekeeper and a widow Hollier living on Parish Relief. The census returns of the 19th century also show that there were cordwainers, boot makers, a George Dyer and finally a widow Harriet Chauve, aged 71, living on her own means. Whether these tenants paid rent to the Burges Family is not clear.

Elderly villagers say that they remember two unmarried ladies, who were seamstresses, living in Rose Cottage in the 1960s.

In 1890 Betsy Painter-Wilmott sold the cottage to Sarah Burges for £50 and in 1953 Albert Fisher, a carpenter, who appeared to own a considerable amount of land in Churchill and Langford, sold the property to Thomas Garrett.

The property changed hands again in 1974 when Charles William Orange sold it to Dr Rafferty for £11,250. Dr Rafferty and his wife, Pamela, only lived in the cottage for two years when he built the integral garage and discovered the inglenook fireplace. Dr & Mrs Rafferty sold the property to Mr & Mrs Peter Broughton in 1975. Mr & Mrs Simpkins then purchased it. Peter Simpkins was a wildlife photographer for the BBC and he and his wife had the extension built around 1983. The current owner, a social worker, bought the cottage in 1987 for £70,000 and hopes to end her days within its walls.

-8-

Dring Cottage

Jo Fryer

Dring Cottage is a Georgian house which was previously called Burgesville. It was once a shop and at one time possibly had a rope factory operating from its outbuildings.

Dring Cottage is a listed building and is described as having a probable late 17th century core with early 19th century additions and a 20th century slate roof. It is believed to have been built by Richard Burges, a plasterer and tiler, but it is possible that he may have rebuilt an existing house. On the suggestion of his grandson, Richard he named it Burgesville.

The present owners are Rebecca and Andrew Wimshurst. Fortunately for our research, Rebecca was visited by the great, great granddaughter of Richard Burges who gave her a transcript of her grandfather's notes about the Burges family.

Our first Richard Burges married three times. He met his third wife, Sarah, a Churchill girl, while she was waiting for a coach at Langford. The grandson of Richard and Sarah Burges, also a Richard, wrote in his autobiographical notes, "*This Churchill lass came up in frolic to meet the coach from Bath and this, they say, is how they met.*"

In the 1841 Census Richard Burges was 50 and was married to Sarah 45. Their children are Ellen 16, James 13, Sarah 10, William 7, Ann 4 and Mary 2. Sarah and Richard had a large family and it is reputed that three of their children died on the same day through an epidemic. Evidence has been found showing that two daughters, Ann age 5 years 11 months and Mary aged 3 years 11 months, died on the same day in 1842.

In 1851 Richard is shown as 68 and is described as a master painter and plasterer. Richard has not really aged 18 years in ten years as census returns rounded ages to the nearest 5 years and were not renowned for their accuracy! His wife, Sarah is shown as 56 and their children are James 23 a journeyman, plasterer and painter, Sarah 20 and William 17.

For reasons we do not know, Sarah Burges's father had 'cut her off' with just one shilling (5p) to her name. Her brother, who was much better off, asked her if she would bother doing anything with the shilling. Her reply was that she would not spend it until she was bound to do so.

After a 'little tiff' with her husband, Sarah Burges was determined to open a shop. It was to sell anything and everything and became so well known for its remarkable range of stock that people would put them to the test by asking for things they would not expect to be in stock! There were regular supplies brought from Bristol and London and Sarah Burges went to London herself once or twice a year to buy stock.

Her grandson, Richard, reports that "*Little by little she saved and little by little she invested in land etc. Thus the 1 shilling remained unspent in the safe.*"

Richard became great friends with his grandmother. He would do odd jobs for her and once made her a gate. His main task was to look after the poultry and the garden.

Richard recollects, "*How well I recall the old lady, with unsteady hand, measuring out the flour, rice, sugar, tea, coffee. From her nose would drop an occasional crystal drop which*

I watched with great interest. She ground the coffee beans and set me to help. I liked my little jobs to be near the sweets where I could pinch some chocolates. I liked those about the size of a penny with small specks of white sugar on them."

She never used that shilling. The coin was dated 1817 from the reign of George III. It was mounted in a silver rim and was kept in the family safe. It was passed through the family and when her grandson, Richard Burges, inherited it he attached it to his watch chain.

During Sarah and Richard's time at Burgesville (Dring Cottage) and long after their children had married and 'gone out into the world' the house was used as a family 'hospital'. Richard's brother, James, was 'very thin and 'wasting terribly' and was sent to Burgesville to recouperate. He was set to work instead of being carefully nursed and when Richard and his mother visited him they found him 'ready to die', and took him back home to Wales. He died aged thirteen and his mother was probably close to the truth when she said, 'Langford killed the lad.'

By 1861 Sarah Burgess [note new spelling of Burges] was a widow of 66 and the census return described her as a shopkeeper. Her daughter Sarah Sabina, aged 30 was living with her and her occupation is stated as housework.

By 1871 Sarah Burgess remained head of the household and was still running her shop. Her daughter Sarah Sabina, aged 40 was living with her as was her granddaughter Ada Kitley, aged 7.

Sarah Sabina Burges

Richard reports that there was a large house (known as Hylsbroke now Milfort) next to Burgesville and a public path called the Dring separating the two properties. A promise was made that the gentleman in the large house should keep the trees cut and the Dring in order. It was a verbal promise and was never kept. Richard says, *"Burgesville is now bounded on the side by the Dring, a filthy place and a hiding place for undesirables."*

The Burges family had a pew in Burrington Church. Richard's father, William, was an organ blower there. Richard would go to Burrington Church with his Aunt Sarah Sabina. They also attended Church at Churchill but Richard states that he favoured the local Congregational Church most. Richard became a temporary Pastor of Wrington and Langford Churches after his return from India in December 1921 and continued this until November 1925.

In 1881 Sarah Burgess is described as a general shopkeeper of 86 and her daughter Sarah Sabina aged 50, a shopkeeper's assistant. Her grandson Frank Kitley aged 28, a painter, is also living there.

Richard Burgess wrote about the death, in 1884, of his grandmother, aged 90.

> *"I had great difficulty getting permission to attend the funeral. I was not so anxious to go but I was quite overdone with long hours and begged for a short respite. To Langford therefore I went. The funeral was quite an event because Grandma was ninety years of age and had lived in Burgesville since her marriage. I was like a caged bird set free and I am sorry to recall that I acted with some levity. It was wet and cold. We were all put in an open top coach. Uncle James Burges, Cardiff, was near me. I guided the cold drops of rain into his ear from my umbrella ribs. He was startled and showed it. I was tickled but tried not to show it!!"*

The census return of 1891 shows Sarah Sabina Burgess, aged 60 to be living on her own means at Dring Cottage. She has a visitor at the time of the census who is Shadrack Gowen aged 17 and a scholar.

It is not yet known who occupied Dring Cottage in the 1900s.

No evidence has been found to confirm that Dring Cottage was once a rope factory or even a date for this. It has been suggested that the length of the outbuildings would have been very suitable for this use.

In more recent times Dring Cottage has been occupied by Mrs Hudson who in February 1961 set up the Langford Women's Institute (WI).

It was bought by Mr and Mrs Harrison who then sold it to Mr and Mrs Thomn. Today it is the home of Andrew and Rebecca Wimshurst and their family.

-9-

Alden House

Alex Kolombos

A Grade II 1820s late Regency house with outbuildings and the addition of a substantial Victorian wing, Alden House is set in its own 2.3 acres surrounded by fields owned by the University of Bristol. The house originally built as a Gentleman's residence was part of a farm complex in late Victorian times, before its more recent association with the University from 1952 to 1980.

Alden House is the current name (since 1980) of the property formerly known as Mendip View (from 1890s to 1980) and before that as Mendip Villa (from 1841 census and the 1838 Tithe map). The new owner of the house in 1980 wanted a unique house name to avoid confusion with the numerous other Mendip Views and so chose a family name, Alden, for the house.

The house that stands today, originally a lime rendered, double-gabled Regency, appears to have been built around the early 1820s as a Gentleman's residence. A grand entrance with a sweeping staircase, mahogany handrail, reeded balusters and oak floor boards, and an elegant curved walled drawing room are highlighted in the listing. Flag stones, old terracotta tiles, a bread oven and a granite fireplace would seem to indicate the addition of a scullery around the 1830s. Drain maps from about this time also show the outbuildings; a shoe house, stable, coach house, chaff house, pig sty and cow house, some of which would from an examination of roof trusses appear to predate the main house. The 1838 Tithe map shows an L- shaped building, probably the original double gable with the scullery addition. Finally, in the 1880s a significant Victorian wing was added to the east of the property when the property appears to have reverted from a Gentleman's residence to a farm complete with a working dairy. The footprint from the 1885 OS surveyor's map is very close to today's site map.

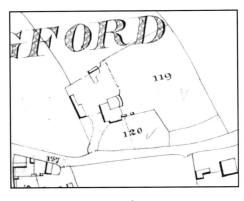

1838 Tithe Map

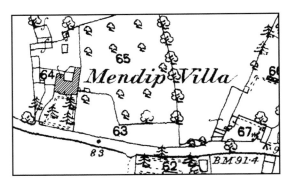

1885 OS map

From a study of earlier maps, and an examination of the land tax records for Burrington back to 1767, it would appear that earlier buildings may have occupied the site, although no evidence of their existence remains today. The land was owned by the Lovell family, but with various occupiers listed.

Since the first edition of this book was published a series of deeds and documents relating to Alden House have been discovered at the University of Bristol Library. The earliest of these dates from 1798 and refers to the 'release and appointment of messuage and premises' dated 31 January 1798, Revd. and Mrs. Whalley to John Naish and trustee. The property is then bought by Richard Wood, a carpenter, from Whalley on 29 September 1801. In the same year Joseph Lovell, a Bristol builder, purchases land and buldings from Richard Wood for £685. There follows an additional appointment and release of premises in March 1806 from Richard Wood to Joseph Lovell. It is quite possible that the transformation of Alden House, by the Lovells, applying their building skills, from a cottage to a more substantial Regency house occurs at this time.

On Joseph's death, his son Lewis Lovell inherits the property. He leaves the property to his son, Joseph Lucas Lovell who inherits the property in 1832 on turning 21.

It is Joseph Lucas Lovell who is listed in the 1841 Census as owner and occupier with his wife Ann, and their two children John and Fanny. Two other children had died in childbirth, reflecting the high rate of infant mortality at the time. In addition, three servants, Jane Usher, Harriet Collins and Edwin Berry are also recorded as living in Mendip Villa. The Lovells were major land owners in the village and the house included just over 8 acres at the time of the census. There are a number of references to Lovells in Langford and Churchill the earliest going back to 1549.

It is apparent that Joseph Lucas has money problems. His wife, Ann dies in 1844. He borrows £400 against the property from Thomas Rogers, an hotelier from Weston, in 1846, and a further £450 two years later from K&I Moore. He eventually sells the house in 1850 to Richard Mills for £1500, and by 1851, he has remarried and moved to Bedminster. He subsequently has three children by his new wife, Harriet, and by the 1861 Census he is described as "Formerly Postman" dying soon after in 1864.

At the time of buying Alden House, Mills owns a number of properties in Langford including Hylesbroke. There is no evidence that he ever lived at Alden House, eventually selling the house in 1872 to Edward Gallop, a local farmer, for £2470.

The earliest legal document in my possession is for a mortgage dated 16th October 1874 in which the new owner, Edward Gallop, borrowed £1000 from a Clevedon widow born in Langford, Elizabeth Mary Swymmer Bird, to secure the property and surrounding land. A reconveyance agreement shows that the money was paid back in full with interest on 6th October 1883. By this time the property is recorded as including over 23 acres, and was probably seen as an attractive purchase by Edward Gallop, who already owned the neighbouring Lodge Farm, to develop his farming interests in the village. These were further enhanced when Sarah, one of Edward's two daughters, married George Crease Hardwick who owned Stepping Stone Farm (now known as Stepstones Farm). They later moved to Havyatt Farm. In her old age Sarah was cared for by Mercy Davy, who sadly died in September 2006, but was one of Langford's oldest living residents.

For a brief period at the end of the 19th century, between them the Gallops and Hardwicks would have owned much of the land to the east of the brook and bounded to the south by the present A38. Today much of this land is now owned by the Wills, the University and Alvis Bros.

When Edward Gallop died in 1898, Mendip View was left to his daughters Sarah and Mary as life tenants. During this time a number of tenants are recorded in Kellys as having lived at the house including Mrs Danger and Dr Ernest Pineo, who ran his medical practice from Mendip View for a brief time before the First World War, and William Vincent Wood, a surgeon, When Sarah died in 1952, the house was sold for £4,700 to Professor Blakemore of the University Of Bristol Veterinary School with 2.3 acres surrounding the property, while the University retained the rest of the land, about 33 acres, for stock. Blakemore died in 1955, and his widow, Rachel, sold the house to the University for use by the Farm Estate manager and his wife, the McCreas.

At this time in the 1950s, the University was busy expanding in the village from its original purchase of Langford House to include the purchases of Langford Place, The Old Post Office, and Mendip View. Subsequently by the early 1980s, some of these properties were sold on by public auction, although the University still retained much of the land for its stock.

Since 1980, Mendip View/Alden House has remained in private hands. In 1987 as part of a major revision of listed buildings, the house was Grade II listed with several internal features protected.

In the front garden, there stands a large yew tree, with its lower branches forming a clipped hedge. With a girth of some 16 ft, the tree could be some 300 to 400 years old, possibly one of the oldest living trees in the village. Another interesting feature in the garden is the high limestone wall surrounding two sides (N and E) of the orchard. It is clearly shown on the 1838 Tithe map and along with the limestone walls of the house would have been constructed from stone transported from the Mendips.

Recent visitors to Alden House have included two sisters, currently living in Wrington, related to George Hardwick, who recalled visiting the property as young children in the 1920s. It was fascinating to watch as their memories took them back to recollections of summer houses and hide and seek games around the house and garden.

-10-

Milfort/Hylesbroke

(formerly Langford Lodge, Hylesbrook, Haylesbrook and Hylsbroke)

Jill Hale

Since the 1950s, Milfort/Hylesbroke, has been two distinct properties although usually under one ownership. Milfort is the Georgian part of the property whilst Hylesbroke, the service wing and a Victorian addition, is now divided into 3 flats.

*A Victorian artist's impression of 'Hylesbroke' with Mendip Lodge in the background
(See Colour Plate 13, page 117)*

This property is situated in Lower Langford between the by-pass and the road that runs through the village. It was built about 1820 by Benjamin Somers on a site believed to have been previously occupied by a farmhouse, hence its imposing elevated position. The property has two vaulted cellars which possibly date from the 1820s. One is now the wood store and the other contains the original wine racks. However, one of the other cellars has a window-like aperture, approximately 104 x 104 x 76cm (41 x 41 x 30in), which could be the outside wall of the original building.

It has had several names, firstly being called Langford Lodge until the 1870s, then Hylesbrook/Hylsbroke/Hylesbroke, probably taking its name from the stream running near the property and the break in the Mendip Hills on the south side. A copy of a Royal Charter dated 904AD, confirming the granting of the Manor of Wrington to Duke Ethelfrith by the Anglo Saxon King Edward, describes part of the boundary as follows, '*From Elkanlegh to Hylisbrok to the Great Spring, then along the brook once more to the Wring*'. A Charter of the Manor of Banwell dated 1065AD describes the same boundary in the opposite direction '*to the Wrinnaest Stream, on till it comes to Hillsbrook, up till it comes to the large spring. First at the large spring of Hillsbrook, east to the Cumbe, and all round Losa Lea*'. However, the Georgian section is now known as Milfort.

Milfort was placed on the North Somerset Register of Listed Buildings, Grade II, in 1987 and comprises a large detached house divided into two distinct sections. The main house, reached via the easterly side of an oval drive to the northern elevation, has a projecting semi-circular portico of Tuscan columns with Ionic capitals with deep entablature and dentil frieze. The main doorway comprises a reeded, segmental-headed architrave with a six panelled, two-leaf door and segmental patterned fanlight. Above the central upper window is a plaster plaque with decorative swags. The south front has a nine bay lean-to ironwork verandah with pointed Gothick openings and scrolled piers and tall ground floor French windows with marginal glazing. These windows did have outside shutters but these were removed for repair by a previous owner. The north front has twelve pane sashes in splayed surrounds.

Tuscan Columns with Ionic Capitals

Entablature and Dentil Frieze
(See Colour Plate 15, page 118)

Inside the main house a cantilevered staircase, with cast iron balusters and lion masks and floral sprays, rises to the first floor. The doorways have reeded architraves with paterae roundels and octagonal panels. The rooms have anthemion and acanthus frieze cornices and there is a marble chimneypiece in one of the ground floor reception rooms.

Paterae roundels & octagonal panelling
(See Colour Plate 16, Page 118)

Anthemion & acanthus frieze

Cast iron balusters & lion mask
& floral sprays
(See Colour Plate 14, Page 118)

The service wing, which was a later addition, has a mixed sashed fenestration and a 2-storey pyramidal roofed tower to the southwest corner. This section of the house retains the name 'Hylesbroke' and was converted into four flats, two on the ground floor and two on the first floor. However, in the 1990s one of the ground floor flats was taken back into the main house as extra living/office accommodation.

In 1841 the property was occupied by Thomas Bumpsted, 40, a Clerk in Holy Orders, and curate at Burrington, his wife Frances 40 and five male fifteen-year-old pupils together with five servants. By 1851 he had three pupils and three resident female servants. Thomas Bumpsted owned parcels of land numbered 126, 127, garden offices & lawns, 128 paddock, 129, 130 & 131 swampy or suggey ground, 132 an orchard, 133 locks and 134 arable/pasture land as recorded on the tithe map and Instrument of Apportionment and Book of Reference, paying a total rent charge of £8. 0s 10¾ d. The property was conveyed, on the 25th March 1846, by Revd. Alfred Smith (by direction of the Revd. Thomas Jeffery Bumpsted and Frances his wife), to Richard Mills, 57, an annuitant, who was born in Hadleigh, Suffolk and a retired Bombay East India Civil Servant. It is believed the property was part of a Settlement dated 13th April 1820 upon the marriage of Thomas Bumpsted and Miss Frances Smith.

To enlarge the estate in 1851, Richard Mills purchased from Mr Samuel Blake of Gosport & others, (trustees of the estate of Abraham Naish), parcels of land numbered 124, the land to the side and rear of the Langford Inn and land numbered 121, the land directly opposite the main gates of Hylesbroke, for the sum of £1,028.0.8d. George Price Esq., who owned St. Mary's House and later bought Richmond House, had purchased the land from Samuel Blake and others for £900.0.0d., but sold it to Richard Mills for £1,028.8.0d. Richard Mills paid £900.0.0d. to the trustees and £128.8.0d. to George Price. He lived in the house with his wife, Eugenia, a British Subject who was born at sea, his son Richard and one male and three female servants.

Signatures of Samuel Blake and Richard Mills
(See Colour Plate 18, Page 120)

By an Indenture dated 26th December 1878 the property was conveyed by Evan Henry Llewellyn Esq. of Langford Court to the Revd. Francis Felix Marie Fortunatus Mazuchelli, for the sum of £4,400. E. H. Llewellyn Esq. had purchased the property from Richard Mills' widow, Eugenia, on the 25th March 1875. The title conveyed totalled 25 acres, 1 rood and 9 perches and was numbered on the Tithe Commutation Map 126 – the mansion house and the land to the north of the house, 127, 128 & 132 – the land to the south, and 124 – the land behind and to the side of the Langford Inn and where eventually Nos. 1 & 2 The Bridge would be erected, as well as 126 – the land directly to the front of the house on the north side. There is a proviso in this deed as follows '......
Francis Felix Marie Fortunatus Mazuchelli doth hereby declare that his Widow if one shall survive him shall not be entitled to dower out of or in the said tenements and hereditaments'.

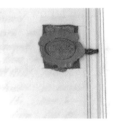

Signature of E. H. Llewellyn
(See Colour Plate 21, Page 122)

Signature of F. F. Mazuchelli
(See Colour Plate 19, Page 120)

Land numbered 121 was the subject of a separate Indenture dated 23 March 1872 between Richard Mills and Edward Gallop and land numbered 122 and 123 was conveyed by another Indenture, of the same date, by Richard Mills to John Gadd.

Richard Mills must have been a philanthropist as in a book written by Evan Henry Llewellyn on Burrington there is a reference to '*the pump, nearly opposite the school, probably was erected over the parish well, and was, as the brass plate attached to it relates, the gift of Mr Mills of Langford Lodge, (now called Hylsbroke). A few years ago, owing to its being found after many attempts impossible to keep the well clear of sewage, the pump handle was removed to prevent the children drinking the impure water'*. Unfortunately, only the rivets remain which attached the plaque to the pump.

The Revd. Mazuchelli mortgaged the property on the 14th January 1879 to a Mrs Mary James, a widow of Wrington, to secure £1,200 upon which interest was due at the rate of four pounds per centum per annum payable half yearly on the 14th January and 14th July. The Revd. Mazuchelli also covenanted to insure the property *'from loss or damage by fire in the joint names of Mary James and him…. ….. in the sum of one thousand pounds at the least in the Sun Insurance Office or some other Office for Insurance to be approved ……. `*

The Revd. Mazuchelli was born in Siena, Northern Italy on the 15th December 1820 and ordained in 1845 in the U.S.A. He received an honorary degree of Doctor of Divinity at St. Mary's College in 1849 which suggests that his family had emigrated to America. He became a naturalised British Subject in 1856 and was a Senior Chaplain in the Indian Army until his retirement in 1878 when he purchased 'Milfort', then known as 'Hylsbroke'. He married Nina (Sarah Elizabeth, nee Harris, 1832-1914), a notable traveller, in Geneva on the 20th August 1853. He served in a succession of parishes in London and the South of England before becoming a chaplain in the Army of the East India Company.

During his time in Darjeeling they undertook, a two-month journey to the Himalayas, covering 1000 km and travelling at altitudes of up to 3800 metres, going above the level of permanent snow, nearly reaching the Tibetan border. Nina's subsequent book, which she also illustrated, was entitled 'The Indian Alps and how we crossed them' by a Lady Pioneer. However, her identity was known to the British Museum. A little later on they made a long journey into Hungary, Slovakia and Transylvania, visiting the Carpathian Mountains. Her book on this subject was entitled 'Magyarland' by a 'Fellow of the Carpathian Society'. After their time in Langford, where Francis assisted with the services at Wrington, they moved to Felmersham near Bedford. It was here that Francis became Vicar from 1889-1895 until his retirement to Nantgaredig, near Carmarthen, Wales where he died on the 15th March 1901. Nina remained there until her death on the 24th January 1914. They were both buried at Burrington where there is a memorial to them and also her mother, Rachel Harris. She left a large sum of money to the Burrington Parish for charity.

Fig. 3. A self-portrait of Elizabeth Mazuchelli during the Himalayan expedition of 1870 – 1871, from p. 293 of her book *The Indian Alps and how we crossed them*[10]

Their occupancy only lasted about six years and on the 25th March 1884 the Revd. Mazuchelli and Evan Henry Llewellyn conveyed the property to Captain John Tyssen (1812-1893). The property was mortgaged on the 26th March 1884 by Capt. John Tyssen, R.N., retired, to Capt. John Tyssen, The Revd. John Yelloly and Frederick Halsey Janson Esq., for the sum of £5,600. However, in 1888 the property was re-conveyed to Capt. John Tyssen and his son, Hugh Samuel Tyssen. Capt. John who had been born at Narborough Hall, Norfolk occupied the property with his wife Mary Jane, nee Lonsada, and his daughters Eleanor and Gertrude, with a lady's maid, cook and housemaid in attendance. They had married in 1864 at Honiton, Devon. His first marriage to Eleanor Margaret Yelloly had taken place at Sudbury, Suffolk in 1850. On the 1891 Census Return Capt. John was registered as blind.

Signatures of John Tyssen and John Yelloly

Signature of Hugh Samuel Tyssen
(See Colour Plate 20, Page 121)

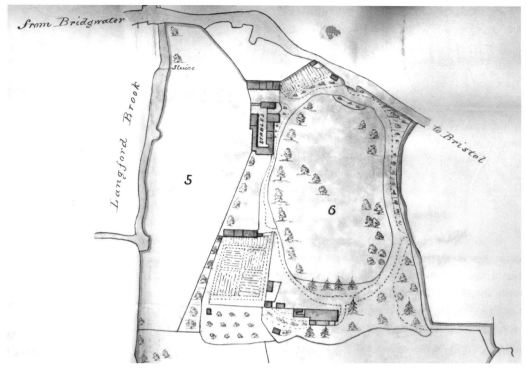

Plan taken from Mortgage dated 26ᵗʰ March 1884
(See Colour Plate 17, Page 119)

By 1901 the property was occupied by Hugh Samuel Tyssen (1868-43) together with his wife, Emily and two female servants. Before the Second World War Hugh Samuel was Master of the Mendip Hunt and drove to the Castle of Comfort, where his horses were kept, as he hunted three days a week in season. Tennis parties were held on the Tennis Court on the northeast corner of the property with local people taking part, including Dr. Pineo's daughters. After dinner parties, the gentlemen would retire to the billiard room, now part of one of the flats, and the ladies would join them to view the game from a raised area where banquette type seating was installed.

During the last 60 years the property has had a variety of owners, ranging from a market gardener, a solicitor, a company director, a radiologist and latterly a dental surgeon and his wife, a headmistress. However, the family with the longest tenure was the Tyssen's, who occupied the property from 1884 until 1945.

The Tyssens were landed gentry of independent means. During their occupation the cellars beneath the property were used for wine and the cellar on the eastern side was a dairy where Mrs Olive Williams, the cook, with twenty-five years' service, made butter on Mondays and Thursdays, from the milk of a pedigree herd of Guernsey cows. The truckles of cheese were also stored in the cellar and the whey was used to feed the few pigs on the estate.

'Mr Eric Buxton, late of 'Glendower', Langford Lane, looked after the cows and was the only person who could handle the herd's two bulls, *'Gaylad'* and *'Slogan of Claverham'*. When he was called up in 1940 for the R.A.F., the bulls had to be sold. Subsequently the butler, Mr George Williams, the cook's husband and Mr Hugh Tyssen, owner, looked after the kitchen garden as part of the war effort.

The day started very early for the staff in the house. At 6.45 a.m. the house parlour maid would take Mrs Tyssen a glass of hot water to her bedroom, which was on the northeast corner of the house. The Tyssens ate lavishly, being supplied with meat from the butcher at Wrington, wine from Oakhill Brewery and fruit and vegetables from the well-stocked walled garden. Besides the usual vegetables, the garden had two soft fruit cages, peach, pear, fig, quince, apple and medlar trees as well as greenhouses providing tomatoes and cucumbers.

A cooked breakfast was served at 9.00 a.m., lunch at 1.00 p.m. and a four course dinner at 7.30 p.m. as well as afternoon tea for which two cakes were made. One had to be 'sad', i.e. the cook would depress (punch) the centre of the cake, as Mr Hugh liked his cake soft. Cooking was carried out on a solid fuel stove that provided hot running water for the family. The staff's day ended when everything had been cleared away and washed up after dinner, with the silver being returned to the safe, which was kept in the pantry.

The staff had Sunday mornings free and also every other Sunday afternoon/evening. On their days off they had to be back by 10.00pm, entering through the front door and reporting directly to the Tyssens, whom they addressed as sir or madam, to let them know of their return.

The servants' quarters were sparsely furnished and the staff were required to purchase their own uniforms which consisted of a black dress with white muslin cap and apron for the afternoons and a check dress, with large white apron and cap for the mornings. Both were worn with black shoes and stockings. The butler wore a dark suit, white shirt and bow tie with black shoes, and with a check apron in the mornings. The cook and the butler jointly earned £16 per month. Mrs Audrey Plumley of Burrington worked in the house as a house parlourmaid from 1939-41 earning £0.14.0d. per week.

Mr Hugh Samuel Tyssen died in 1943 and was laid to rest, as was his wife Emily, on the south side of Burrington Churchyard. His son, Air Vice Marshal John Hugh Samuel, known as Jack, (1889-1953) served during the 1914-18 war in France with the North Somerset Yeomanry and transferred to the Royal Flying Corps and actually landed his aircraft in one of the fields adjacent to the house. Following a long service career, which included spells in India and Iraq, he finished his service in 1942 as an Air Officer Commanding No. 16 Group, Chatham 1940-41 and is featured in four paintings held by the National Portrait Gallery. From 1942-45 he was with the North Eastern Civil Defence Organisation. His wife was a very beautiful lady and his son, Michael John Hugh Samuel, also served in the Second World War.

Following Hugh Samuel Tyssen's death, Mrs Emily Tyssen remained in residence, with part-time domestic help, until November 1945 when the property was sold to the Harris Family and the fields to Mrs Webb of Wyndhurst Farm. The Auction Sale, which lasted three days, was in the hands of Mr Percy Palmer of Weston-super-Mare with the Police in attendance to guard 3,000 ounces of silver.

During the Harris' occupation a chauffeur drove Mrs. Harris around in a Rolls Royce. Her daughter, Dorothy, had a room in the Hylesbroke side of the property and returned to Winscombe Hall for weekends. Her son, George, fell in love with Madge Browning, whose brother was joint proprietor of Messrs. Browning & Watt, the General Stores on the A38 near the Churchill Inn. She had lived at Nash House as a child, and had promised her parents not to leave home until their deaths. She was 36 when she married George and they took up residence at Hylesbroke and later had a bungalow ('Harbrow', an amalgam of Harris and Browning) built on the rick yard on the westerly side of the oval drive.

On the 2nd December 1952 the main house, with 6.059 acres, was sold to Mr Peter Gibb, a solicitor with practices in Bristol and Axbridge, and his wife, Susan. The price paid was £5,300 and their occupation lasted for twenty-five years. During this time Mr & Mrs Gibb lined the easterly drive with sweet chestnuts and renamed the main house 'Milfort' after a property of the same name at Portlaw, near Waterford in the Republic of Ireland, the home of the Morley-Malcolmson Family where Mrs Gibb (nee Morley) had spent many happy childhood holidays. The property was the subject of a Compulsory Purchase Order for land to straighten out the road on the south side and as a result of that order the local council planted a row of trees to act as a noise barrier from the A38. They subsequently purchased the westerly side of the property, which had been divided into four flats.

Mr Gibb was the Chairman of the Governors of Westwing School situated at Langford Court. The school moved to Tockington in 1960 when the Wills family returned to Langford. For a couple of years a kindergarten was run by Miss Young, a former teacher at Westwing, in one of the Hylesbroke flats to fill the gap for several local families caused by the school's move.

Their daughters Joanna and Rosemary have many happy memories of the house and recall helping Mrs Madge Harris with the pricking out of the seedlings in the Nursery Garden. Great use was made of the Tennis Court, which was refurbished during 1953-54. Rosemary remembers that the cellars, which were used for storage, were great fun for playing in and for parties. One had a table tennis table in it and there was a wooden contraption in another which consisted of two long rough poles, which she was told were used for rolling down the milk churns down.

Following Rosemary's marriage, her parents sold the property to a company director, Mr Roger Champion who re-roofed the house himself and, with his wife's help, completely repainted both the render and woodwork on the outside of the house, built a raised terrace with balustrading on the south side, with steps down to the garden and refurbished the tennis court, as his wife was a keen tennis player. Sadly, he was killed in a car accident on the A370 in February 1983.

The next owners were Dr. & Mrs J. Virjee, a consultant radiologist and his wife and five children. During their time, the stables and dressage ring were built as their children were keen riders and one of their daughters, Lucinda, represented her country at junior level in dressage.

The property was then sold to its present owners, Mr Paul & Mrs Alison Norcross, a dental surgeon and his wife, a head teacher. Mr & Mrs Norcross have now reinstated the conservatory on the south elevation to great effect. The original structure had to be pulled down during the harsh winter of 1962/3 when snow from the main roof fell onto it.

Throughout its long history there has been a strong link with the clergy. In the 1840s Thomas Bumpsted was Curate at Burrington. Richard Mills' wife, Eugenia, was the daughter of a minister and in the late 1870/early 1880s the Revd. Mazuchelli was helping with the services at Wrington. In the twentieth & twenty-first centuries Latterly Mr Peter Gibb was a churchwarden and Mr Paul Norcross is a lay preacher.

The Porters Lodge, mentioned on a deed in 1884, is now known as Hylesbroke Lodge. On the 1901 Census Return it was occupied by Stephen & Annie Day and their daughter Laura. It was condemned by the Axbridge Rural District Council in the middle 1930s when its occupants, Mr George & Mrs Olive Williams and their daughter, Betty, the Tyssen's butler and cook, moved into the 'Big House'. In the early 1940s the Lodge was requisitioned as a dwelling for evacuees. It was sold by the Mrs Harris' to George Henry Butler on the 25th September 1952 for the sum of £1,850 and has had four subsequent owners.

The bungalow erected for Mr & Mrs George Harris on the westerly side of the property in the 1950s was later extended to accommodate Mrs Harris' sister Maud Thatcher and her husband. Its size has made it conducive to dual occupation.

The adjacent farm buildings have also been converted into three dwellings, as has the old coach house/stables to the main house in the 1970s/early 1980s. The Potting Shed and walled garden is a separate dwelling having been converted in the early 21st century.

Although the various properties within the Milfort/Hylesbroke complex are individually owned and no longer part of a large self-sufficient estate, there is a strong sense of community and each individual property has been carefully renovated, enhancing the general ambiance of a bygone era.

-11-

Wistaria House

Graham Perry

Evidence suggests that the earliest building on the site was possibly a two-roomed single-storey cottage. Subsequently, additions were added to the north side, then a two-storey building (shop) on the roadside to the south. Later a two-storey structure was built to infill between the shop and the original cottage which then received an upstairs. Later still a second shop was added at the roadside. In 1979, the two roadside shops were demolished leaving a Georgian-style house.

Ownership

The earliest reference found to ownership shows that around 1790 John Naish purchased the messuage and 15 acres from the Rev. T. S. Whalley and Elizabeth, his wife. Naish and his wife must have died around 1825 as probate was granted on his will in 1826. It can be assumed that Naish predeceased his wife since she left her property to a niece, or failing that, to her brother-in-law, Abraham Naish, a grocer from Romsey, Hants. Her estate was valued at under £300 for probate duty.

In 1830, Abraham Naish sold some land to Benjamin Somers and by the time of the Burrington Tithe Apportionment in 1838, he owned 13 acres. These approximate to the field between the current Wistaria House and Alden House (formerly Mendip View) to the East, the ground on which Brook House stands and the orchard behind, and the field immediately to the West of the Langford Inn. This field was 'occupied' by Thomas Fenwick and was described as pasture. The occupier of the house, identified as Wistaria House (note spelling), was one James Isgar, and in the 1841 Census his occupation was listed as farmer and shopkeeper. This is the first reference to the house name and a shop business.

Naish died in 1849 and, in 1850, his executors sold the 'messuage or dwellinghouse shop land hereditaments' for £500 to Richard Mills. The papers refer only to the land (4 acres 1 rood and 24 perches according to the 1838 Tithe Apportionment), belonging to the present house, Brook House and the orchard behind, so the other two fields must have been sold between 1838 and 1850. At the time of Naish's death, the property was occupied by William Taylor and Mary Bennett as tenants.

In March 1864 Richard Mills sold the messuage, garden and orchard to Mr John Gadd, and in 1872, Elizabeth Swymmer Bird, a widow of Clevedon, took out a mortgage with John Gadd for £400 and became a co-owner. In 1864 the address of Richard Mills was given as Langford Lodge. Richard Mills died in 1874 and his estate was valued at £6000.

In 1884, Elizabeth Bird and John Gadd sold the 'Dwelling house and shop and outbuildings garden and orchard hereditaments' to Henry Wilkins of Langford for £800 and Elizabeth Bird and John Gadd each received £400. The land purchased by Henry Wilkins consisted of 4 acres, 1 rood and 24 perches (more or less) so it would appear that no land was sold between 1850 and 1884. Henry Wilkins had to take out a mortgage for £500 with Elizabeth Bird at 4% per annum and had to pay interest half yearly on any money which remained owing.

Nothing is known about the type of shop previously run but an advertisement in the Parish Magazine for 1900 shows that Henry Wilkins was proprietor of a large business with a range of stock items that would grace a modern city store, a garden centre and a farmers' merchants!

HENRY WILKINS,

Draper, Hosier, Outfitter, Hatter, Family Grocer, Ironmonger, Corn, Meal & Provision Merchant,

THE STORES, LANGFORD.

Hosiery, Drapery, Ladies' Jackets, Haberdashery, &c., selected from the best
London, Manchester, and West of England Warehouses.

Clothing Clubs and Charities Supplied.

Grocery, Drapery, Outfitting & Ironmongery each in separate Departments.
Ironmongery Show Room on Second Floor.

General Outfitter. Suits to Measure, quality according to price. Good Workmanship.

SINGLE GARMENTS TO MEASURE.

Covert and Dust Coats in Meltons, Beavers, Cheviots, Irish Friezes, &c.

Business Suits in all the Newest Designs. Navy Blue Serge Suits. Cord & Moleskin Trousers.
Sleeve Waistcoats and Duck Jackets.

Call and see a choice and varied Selection of Patterns before buying elsewhere.

Electro-Plated Goods. — Best Sheffield Manufacture.

Sponges, Leathers, Housemaids' Gloves, Garden Gloves, Hedging Gloves, Tan Gloves.

Garden and Agricultural Seeds.

Hay Rakes, Bee Hives, Garden Baskets, Wood Taps, Spoons, Rolling Pins, Bread Boards.

Bassinettes, Mail Carts, Perambucottes, Mats, Matting, Floorcloth, Linoleum, Carpets.

Quotations given and Samples sent to compare with any other House.

ORDERS FOR GOODS NOT IN STOCK OBTAINED PROMPTLY.

Brown Ware, Pans, Salting Pans, Bread Pans, Cream Pans, Flower Pots.
Schwepps' Mineral Waters in Bottles and Syphons.

GENERAL FURNISHING AND IRONMONGERY STORES.

Tools, Cutlery, Brooms, Mats, Brushes, Hay Rope, Halters, Cow Ties, Tar Twine. Birmingham & Sheffield Goods

Palliasses, Mattresses & Millpuff. Drugs, Cattle Medicines, Embrocations, Disinfectants.

Petroleum and other Oils, Paints, &c.

Enamelled, Galvanized and Japanned Goods, Lamps, Stoves and Lamp Glasses, Earthenware, Glass and China.

Fancy Articles, Stationery, Perfumes, Tobacco and Cigars, Stephens' Inks,
Pipes, Pouches, Purses, Walking Sticks.

Noted House for Tea, Coffee and Provisions, Crosse & Blackwell's Goods, Hartley & Beach's Preserves.

Ladies', Gents.' and Children's Boots and Slippers in great variety.

Families waited upon for Orders

Advertisement for the Langford Stores, taken from the Parish Magazine, circa 1900.

In 1933 Henry Wilkins sold the 'dwellinghouse shop outbuildings garden and premises comprising part of Tithe 123 and the whole of number 23 on the ordnance map (1931 edition)'. He retired to the newly constructed Brook House, built on the west side of the garden of Wistaria House and retained ownership of the orchard behind the house. Henry Wilkins died in 1941 and the net value of his estate was £13,990-0s-10d. His last remaining spinster daughter, who lived in Brook House, died in 1988, thus ending over 100 years of family residence in, and next to, the same property in Lower Langford.

The new owner of The Stores was Horace Elsworth of Langford, believed to have been an employee of Henry Wilkins, and the land holding now amounted to 0.434 of an acre. The purchase price was £2000.

In 1955 Mr Elsworth sold The Stores for £4000 to Sidney Barnes of Woking in Surrey. There then followed four changes of ownership, each staying a shorter time than their predecessor.

Date	Vendor	Purchaser	Price
~1790	Rev & Mrs Whalley	John Naish	?
1828	Elizabeth Naish	Left property to Abraham Naish (her brother-in-law)	Less than £300
1850	Executors to Abraham Naish	Richard Mills	£500
1864	Richard Mills	John Gadd	?
1872		Elizabeth Bird became a co-owner by granting a £400 mortgage to John Gadd	
1884	Elizabeth Bird & John Gadd	Henry Wilkins	£800
1933	Henry Wilkins	Horace Elsworth	£2,000
1955	Horace Elsworth	Sidney Barnes	£4,000
1964	Mr Barnes	Mr & Mrs Bevan, Liphook, Hants	£6,500
1971	Mr & Mrs Bevan	Mr & Mrs McCartney, Hungerford, Berks	£9,500
1975	Mr & Mrs McCartney	Mr & Mrs Mewse, Farnham, Surrey	£20,700
1978	Mr & Mrs Mewse	Dr & Mrs Perry, Langford	£34,500

Ownership and purchase prices of The Stores.

Ownership of the property did not necessarily identify the residents! An examination of the Census Returns, beginning in 1841, reveals the names of those living in the house, but an early reference shows that in 1818, James Fry was the occupier when the property was owned by Naish.

It would appear from the Census returns that Henry Wilkins ran the grocery business as a tenant before he actually purchased the property from Elizabeth Bird and John Gadd in 1884.

Date	Owner	Tenants (age)	Occupation
1818	John Naish	James Fry	Farmer?
1841	Abraham Naish	James Isgar (65) Ann Isgar (45) John (25) James (17) James Wolf (12) Mary Bennett (56)	Farmer
1851	Richard Mills	James Isgar (76), widower John (35) James Woolf (22), grandson	Farmer Agric, labourer
1861	Richard Mills	Ann Parker (52) ? Thomas Parker (13) ?	Grocer and Post-mistress Scholar
1871	John Gadd	Elizabeth Jenkins (67), widow	Shopkeeper
1881	John Gadd & Elizabeth Bird	Henry Wilkins (27), head Emily (22) Gertrude (7 months)	Grocer
1891	Henry Wilkins	Henry Wilkins (37) Emily (32) Gertrude (10) Ethel (8) Nora (2) Margaret (1)	Grocer
1901	Henry Wilkins	Henry Wilkins (47) Emily (42) Gertrude (20) Ethel (18) Nora (12) Margaret (11) Georgina (9) Edward (7) Charlotte (19)	General grocer Helper

Owners and tenants of the Langford Stores 1841 - 1901

The Buildings

The buildings on the site have undergone many changes since outlines were first noted on the 1841 Tithe map. In the early days, farming and shopkeeping would have taken place simultaneously, although after 1850, the farming activities may have been restricted to growing fruit, almost certainly apples, judged by the few remaining trees in the orchard.

The 1841 Tithe map shows a small building situated parallel to the road. Presumably this was a single storey cottage since no evidence has been found of a staircase leading to an upper floor. The original building probably consisted of two rooms and is readily discernible in the current property. There is a half-glazed door and fanlight halfway along the hall, presumably the original front door. The front wall is 66cm (26in) thick. On the north side there is another half-glazed door which was probably the rear entrance. The frame of this doorway is constructed of rough hewn oak and the sides and the lintels are fixed together with large wooden dowels. The door is made of pine. The back wall is 59cm (23in) thick.

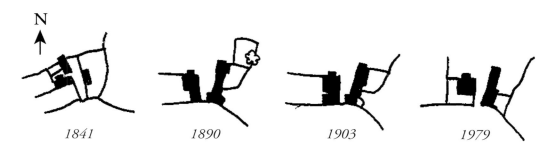

Evolution of the current Wistaria House taken from drawings of the 1841 Tithe map and the 1890, 1903 and 1979 Ordnance Survey maps

It would seem that a room was added later on the north side (this is the attached 'projection' evident on the 1841 map). This could have served as a kitchen since the mains water supply enters through the north wall.

By 1883 an extension had been added to the south side. This may have been constructed in two parts with the part nearest to the road built before the part which connected it to the original cottage. The evidence for this was observed in the disposition of the fireplace and the flue in the southernmost part. They were contained inside the 'new building' adjoining the road. If that is true, then a second phase was then carried out later when the two buildings were joined. This may have been the time when the original east-west orientated single storey building acquired a second floor. The staircase to the upper floor is situated within this 'infill' sector.

The current wall separating the front garden from the yard is the remains of the 'first phase' and the stonework suggested that it was constructed as a two-storey building. There was direct access from the original cottage to the extension but this might only have been facilitated when the infill part was constructed since a doorway was made between the current hallway and the shop.

By 1913, and probably during the early days of Henry Wilkins' ownership, a second double-fronted, single-storey shop was built to the west of the first shop. This was not connected to the house and a pathway existed behind this shop to a front door to the house. The two shops were connected internally. This second shop had large pitch pine pillars supporting the roof trusses.

It is not known when an upper floor and the 'infill' section of the house were constructed. There are two intriguing features to be observed in this part of the property. The staircase contains fourteen steps and then there are two further steps to the left and the right. To the left there is a bedroom and the right turn goes into the landing corridor. The Bristol Georgian House Society suggested that the staircase had not been built for Wistaria House but had been brought from another property and then had to be modified. The second feature concerns the flues. One chimney flue from the north-west corner rises up and turns 90°, crosses the west wall and then bends another 90°, and tracks horizontally across the north wall above the original cottage, with a hatch on the landing, before turning upwards 90° to join in parallel with the other flues. The current lounge fire has

Two of the three king posts supporting the roof

a 2m (78in) horizontal run of flue with an access hatch on the landing to facilitate chimney cleaning. The flues are brick-built rather than stone which might suggest they were added sometime after the main walls were constructed. In the roof space there are four other hatches opening into flues and from the west end to the east they are from the kitchen, dining room and one each from the two drawing rooms. This suggests there were five fireplaces in the house each with its own crown chimney pot.

There are 3 king posts supporting the roof. The two diagonal timbers rising from each appear to be attached at their bases by wooden pegs.

In the mid 1960s a flat roofed extension was built in the north-east corner. This 'squared' off the corner between the original cottage and the first extension on the north side.

In 1979 the new owners demolished the two double-fronted shops. This created a façade to Wistaria House and also a front garden. Only two of the current six features on the front (south) aspect belong to the original 'infill' house. These are the upper and lower windows on the left side of the front aspect. The current front door replaces the two doors present in the 1903 building. The false window above the door was created in 1979. There was almost certainly never a window in that position since there are two cupboards, one in each front bedroom, and a stud and plaster wall immediately behind the false window. The two windows on the eastern side of the front were created when the two-storey shop was demolished. The false window was created to fill in the gap between the upstairs windows and simulate a Georgian façade. This front façade apparently persuaded the local planning authority to confer Grade II listing on Wistaria House in 1987. This action was subsequently reversed in 2001 by the Department of Culture, Media and Sport on the recommendation of English Heritage when it was realised that most features which had persuaded the local planners dated only from 1979.

One other interesting feature emerged during the 1979 alterations. Apparently, when the 'infill' house was built, the upper floor was not exactly aligned, with the result that the post-1979 front wall has a bulge on the eastern end of the South facade!

In 1995 a porch was constructed on the east side leading into the kitchen.

The downstairs flooring appears to have consisted of stone slabs. The current kitchen, looking out onto the yard, had a slab floor resting on earth with a central drain and had probably been used as a dairy at one time. By 1978 it contained a large walk-in refrigerator. Some of the slabs from this room are now inlaid in the front garden path. Elsewhere on the ground floor, with the exception of the room in the south-east corner, the slabs had been covered with asphalt some time before 1978. The south-east corner room had a wood floor which rested on stone piers approximately 40cm (16in) high. This was filled in 1979, and the room now has a solid floor.

The original buildings on the east side of the yard (see 1841 plan) were presumably associated with farming activities, but later became part of the shop enterprise. At the north end there is a three-horse stable with a floor made of blue lias sets and a central drain. Next to that there is currently a large double garage that was probably once a cart shed which was then altered so that the longer motor vehicles could be garaged. Evidence for this is seen in the roof, and roof timbers, facing the yard. It was extended outwards into the yard to make the garage deeper. This could have happened in the 1930s.

Some time between 1841 and 1890 a building was constructed between the cartshed and the road. This was probably used as a store in association with the shop activities. By 1978 this had a corrugated iron roof but it has since been reroofed with pantiles.

The Langford Stores 1978 taken from a painting by Diana Cornish
(See Colour Plate 22, Page 122)

Appendix

The following is reproduced by kind permission of Mrs Hazel Sturgis (neé Elsworth).

'I was born at the house called then, The Stores, in October 1921 and continued to live here until 1947.

I spent a very happy childhood in that house. My sister was 9 years older than me and my brother seven years older, so I was the youngest.

There was a harness room next to the stables and I used to play in there with my dolls etc. It was my little house.

We had lots of cats and kittens as they were supposed to help keep the rats and mice at bay in the 'warehouse' where the meal and corn were stored.

We had no bathroom or toilet and had to go outside to the toilet and when I was little I used to have a bath in front of the kitchen range. In the 1930s my father had a bathroom and toilet put in one of the bedrooms. The only trouble was when it was installed, the pipes went from the kitchen which was the other side of the house, so by the time the hot water got to the bath it was lukewarm.

In those days it was a very cold house. There was a fire in the sitting room and a range in the kitchen, but once you left those rooms it was freezing. The floors, apart from one room, were made of stone slabs. Some of the floors of course had carpet or lino on them.

My bedroom was at the back of the house and sometimes the cats would climb up the roof and sleep on the bed.

We had chickens in the back garden. Lots of fruit bushes, i.e. raspberries, gooseberries etc.

I was married from there in June 1942 but still lived here as, being the war years, my husband was away in the Navy'

-12-

Sutledge House

Trish Coates

Sutledge House and its neighbour Pinkerton House trace their origins to a cottage, which certainly existed in 1841, but in 1869 was extended and converted into a private school.

When, in 1999, John Dunstone, a local builder, hacked off the old render from Sutledge House, Blackmoor, Langford, he was surprised to find the lower roofline of a much older building. The local red conglomerate of the older construction contrasted sharply with large grey blocks of limestone which forms the main part of the building.

This older part of the building, described in various deeds as a 'cottage and garden near the high road leading from Langford to Wrington', comprising 10 acres and 11 perches, was owned by the 'Right Reverend Father in God, George Henry by divine permission Lord Bishop of Bath and Wells'. In 1841 this property was leased to two yeomen brothers, Thomas and Mark Urch of Banwell, but the Census shows that it was occupied by William Counsell (farmer) and his wife Jane. By 1851 William had retired, but he and Jane continued to live there.

Thomas Urch died in 1857, leaving his brother Mark to acquire the estate from the Ecclesiastical Commissioners in 1860 for a mere £40! In the meantime the Counsells either died or moved away and in 1861 Thomas Broadbear, a shoemaker was living there with his wife and three children.

In 1867, Henry George Northover, a local schoolmaster, paid Mark Urch the sum of £300 for the cottage and land. Since 1852 he had been Principal of a boys' boarding school in Lower Langford, probably at Nash House, where the 1861 Census shows 14 boys in residence, together with his wife, three children, his father, Henry Northover and a servant.

It took only two years to build a new school, 'Sutledge House' on the site in Blackmoor, incorporating the cottage. Could the unusual name 'Sutledge' be connected to the river 'Sutlej' now separating India from Pakistan? The Indian mutiny was no doubt fresh in peoples' memories and the Langford Brook, on a slightly smaller scale, babbled through the school's grounds!

The school's prospectus offered 'sons of the middle classes a sound, practical education in one of the most healthy localities in England, delightfully situated and in direct communication with Bristol', with full board and all for 18-20 guineas per annum.

ESTABLISHED 1852.

SUTLEDGE HOUSE,
Middle-Class Commercial Boarding School,
LANGFORD, NEAR BRISTOL.

Principal ... ... Mr. H. G. NORTHOVER.

The above School has been established with a view of providing for the Sons of the Middle Classes, a sound, practical Education, at moderate Terms, and is especially adapted for Youths whose education has been neglected.

The Studies embrace every Branch of Literature requisite to prepare Pupils for a Professional, Commercial, Manufacturing, or Agricultural life, and include :—

[OVER.

School Prospectus (1)

READING AND ELOCUTION
WRITING (Plain and Ornamental)
ARITHMETIC, MATHEMATICS, &c.
MENSURATION (Generally)
LAND SURVEYING (Practically)
GEOGRAPHY, GEOLOGY, ASTRONOMY
ENGLISH GRAMMAR
HISTORIES, LATIN, FRENCH

BOOK-KEEPING, by Single and Double
Entry on the most approved and
modern method, with Commercial
Accounts, Correspondence, Invoices,
Receipts, &c.
DRAWING—Freehand, Geometrical, Archi-
tectural, and Mechanical—gratis
MUSIC AND DANCING

The Pupils may study any or all of the above Branches at the option of their Parents.

The main principle of Teaching is independency; that is, no pupil is kept back for others, none are pushed forward beyond their abilities, nor are any sharp and very quick Boys URGED on for the purpose of gaining a name for the School, and the other Pupils' interests sacrificed or neglected thereby (which three things are too common in the present day), but each receives individual attention, which will give Soundness, Solidity, and Permanence of Acquirement. The number is limited.

Sutledge House was built by Mr. H. G. N., in 1869, for Scholastic purposes, and has accommodations rarely met with in private Schools.

Langford is one of the most healthy localities in England, delightfully situated, and in direct communication with Bristol.

The Pupils are liberally treated, and the most scrupulous attention is paid to their Health, Morals, and Religious Instruction.

Terms:—

Under 11 Years of Age   -   -   -   -   18 Guineas per annum.
Above 11   ,,   ,,   -   -   -
Latin and French (optional)   -   -   per quarter
Music and Dancing   ,,   -   -   -

Washing 8/- per quarter.
Books at Stationers' Prices.

Each Pupil to be provided with dinner knife, four-pronged fork, and dessert spoon. All Linen, &c., to be clearly marked. Linen, &c., for month's wash.

Payments by Quarterly Instalments.

VACATIONS AS USUAL.

PUPILS ACCOMMODATED DURING VACATIONS IF WISHED.
FURTHER INFORMATION WITH PLEASURE.

References:

Mr. ....

Mr. ....

Mr. ....

SUTLEDGE HOUSE,
      LANGFORD, NEAR BRISTOL.

....

Principal.

School Prospectus (2)

When Charles Dickens researched for 'Nicholas Nickleby', which was published in 1839, he travelled to Yorkshire to investigate the conditions and educational methods prevalent in private boarding schools. Mark Ford, a historian, writes about this:

"Although the schools' fulsomely worded newspaper advertisements promised, for only 20 guineas a year, a wide ranging, liberal education that paid particular attention to the 'young gentlemen's' morals, most seem to have been barbarically cruel places in which the boys were starved, flogged and taught little or nothing.,,,,, No doubt some boys were enrolled by credulous parents seduced by the high flown language of the adverts, but the schools appealed also to those looking for a cheap and convenient way of disposing of unwanted or illegitimate offspring. The chilling statement 'No Vacancies' invariably figured in their promotional literature"

Sutledge House was actually cheaper than Dickens' Dotheboys Hall and also offered accommodation during vacations, but hopefully, as the pupils were mostly local, the conditions would not have been so harsh. The 1871 Census lists the following occupants of the house:

Name	Age	Occupation	Where born
Henry Northover	45	School Master	Nunney, Somerset
Eliza Northover	39	Wife	Wrington
Charlotte Northover	17	Governess	Churchill
Walter Northover	14	Scholar	Churchill
Eliza Northover	12	Scholar	Burrington
Alice Northover	4	Scholar	Burrington
Henry Northover	85		Salisbury
Mary Adams	15	Scholar	Shipham
Emma Lidbury	10	Scholar	Congresbury
Matilda Body	8	Scholar	Wrington
Agnes Price	6	Scholar	Allerton
Joseph Biss	13	Scholar	Portishead
Cornthwaite Collins	13	Scholar	Yatton
Edgar Horner	12	Scholar	Newport, Mon
Arthur Horner	10	Scholar	Newport, Mon
Thomas Smith	10	Scholar	Cheddar
Henry Dando	7	Scholar	Wrington
Albert Rich	12	Scholar	Winscombe
William Pool	13	Scholar	Chewton Mendip
John Sage	13	Scholar	East Harptree
William Ralph	14	Scholar	St James', Bristol
Arthur Pearce	14	Scholar	Weston-in-Gordano

It seems that the Northovers were experiencing financial problems. In 1870 they borrowed £350, using the school as security and in 1873 they increased this to £500. Sadly H. G. Northover died in 1877, aged 51 and the school was taken over by his eldest son, Walter, who would have been 18 years old (the crossed out initials can be seen on the schools prospectus). In 1878 Eliza and Walter Northover were forced to increase the mortgage to £600, borrowing from Elizabeth Westlake, a 'Refreshment Housekeeper' from Broadmead, Bristol. Unfortunately they were unable to pay any interest on the capital and the school must have had to close down. The 1881 Census shows only Eliza living in Sutledge House with her daughter Alice (14). Walter had become a tea-dealer, living independently in Blackmoor and was now married with a daughter, Annie. Again, there is only a supposition that the family might have had connections with India.

The house was reclaimed by Elizabeth Westlake and when she died in 1884, her daughter, Marian Rexworthy sold the house for £340 to Naomi Tincknell, a widow from Cox's Green, Wrington who also owned two other properties, numbers 1 and 2 Bakers building, Wrington. She lived in Sutledge House until she died in 1897. In her will, she had appointed Levi Hollier, a local labourer and her sister Hannah Morgan as executors, leaving Sutledge House and all her belongings to them, until her niece, Sarah Edith Morgan had reached 21 years of age. Sarah married George Dennis in 1905 and lived in the house, until she died in 1953, when it was valued at £1,400.

'Touched up' sepia photograph of Sutledge House with the rear part of the house painted out

After 1897, the house entered a new phase of multi-occupancy, when the building was divided up so that various people could occupy different parts. Later, Sarah Dennis' son, George Orlando Dennis, a Memorial sculptor, her son-in-law, Gerald Malpas from Hampshire and Brian John Gosling, a solicitor from Weston-Super-Mare lived in one part of the house and Fredrick William Bartlett, an insurance official from Yeovil lived in the other part. Could this have been the time when it was rumoured that a certain romantic, engineering student used to be constantly distracted from his studies, when he would be forced to sneak up onto the top floor of the house which once had been the boys' dormitory in the Sutledge School days. Here he would be found, gazing intently out of the attic windows across the road in Blackmoor to Brook Cottage, the next house downstream, to where an attractive young lady, who was training to be a school teacher, was living!

Photograph showing original slate roof and Malpas' grandmother at the gate around 1925

In 1958 F. W. Bartlett applied for planning permission for Sutledge House to be converted into a house, 2 flats and a bungalow and the property was valued at £3,000. In 1963 a garage was erected, as well as a bungalow on the site of the old school's wash-room. During this phase, land was sold off and another bungalow was built in the grounds of Sutledge House.

The house survived the great flood of '68, when cars had been hurtled along in the great torrent of water which had swept down Blackmoor. In one of the Sutledge House flats, a lady had to be 'floated' out by the fire brigade to safety! In 1969 F. W. Bartlett sold Sutledge House to George Stone and his wife, Rene, where they brought up their family of four sons, along with some goats and ducks! Rene Stone's parents Arnold and Bessie Derbyshire lived next door in one of the flats and could be reached through an opening made in the wall of the wardrobe in one of the upstairs bedrooms in Sutledge House – almost like another tale from Narnia! The 'pink house by the bridge' became well known in Langford, as many people came into contact with George and Rene Stone through their involvement and good work within the local churches.

Revealing the old chimney

In 2003 it was sold in two lots, Sutledge House to the Coates family from Wrington, who have four daughters, and the flats to Anne McIntyre, who renamed them Pinkerton House. Sutledge House then entered a phase of serious renovations. Wooden sash windows replaced the Crittal steel windows of F. W. Bartlett's era. Damp proofing and re-plastering were tackled and three of the four chimneys were soon in working order. Some of its history was brought to life again, such as when the old school range, which had been blocked off in the past, was exposed and a never-ending deluge of black, acrid-smelling soot filled the room - quite amazing to think this soot could have been almost a century old!

The thick, stone wall separating the North-facing kitchen from another room was knocked down to form a new, larger, lighter kitchen/living room......

Opening up the kitchen

......and those very stones are now being used by a local builder to construct a new cottage in Wrington! If only stones could tell their story...........

Colour Plate Contents

1. Aerial photograph of Lower Langford, 2004

2. Turnpike map of Langford, 1818

3. Door of The Old Post Office, 17th century

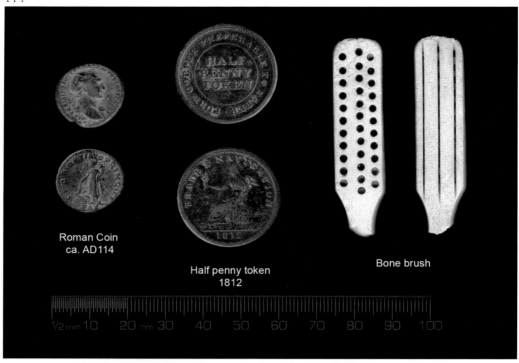

Roman Coin
ca. AD114

Half penny token
1812

Bone brush

4. Finds at Laurel House

5. Limewashes at Laurel House

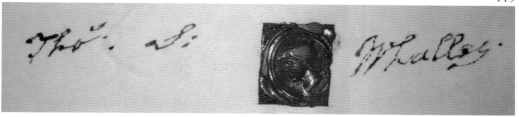

6. Signature of Thomas S. Whalley

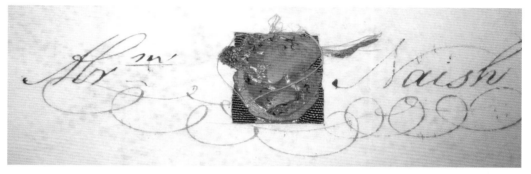

7. Signature of Abraham Naish

8. Signature of Benjamin Somers

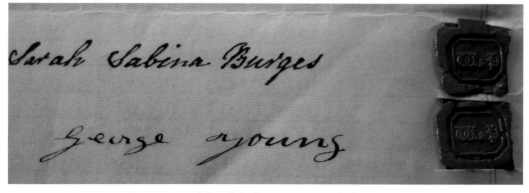

9. Signatures of Sarah Sabina Burges and George Young

10. Apothecary bottles at Rose Cottage

11. Fireplace at Rose Cottage

12. Oven at Rose Cottage

13. Victorian artist's impression of 'Hylesbroke'

14. Cast-iron balusters at Milfort

15. Entablature and dentil frieze at Milfort

16. Paterae roundels & octagonal panelling

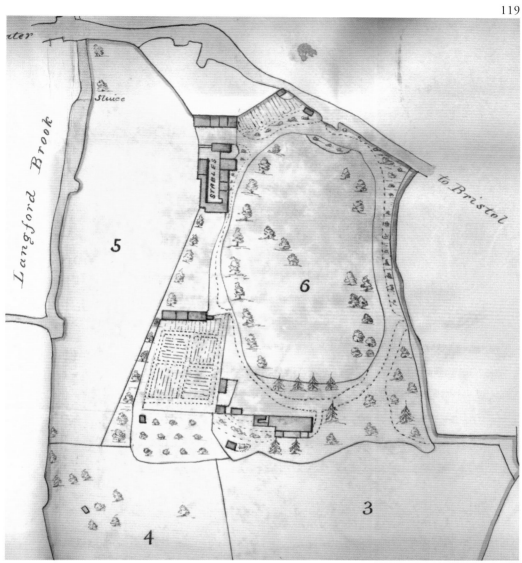

17. Estate map of Milfort, 1884

18. Signatures of George Price and Richard Mills

19. Signature of F. F. Mazuchelli

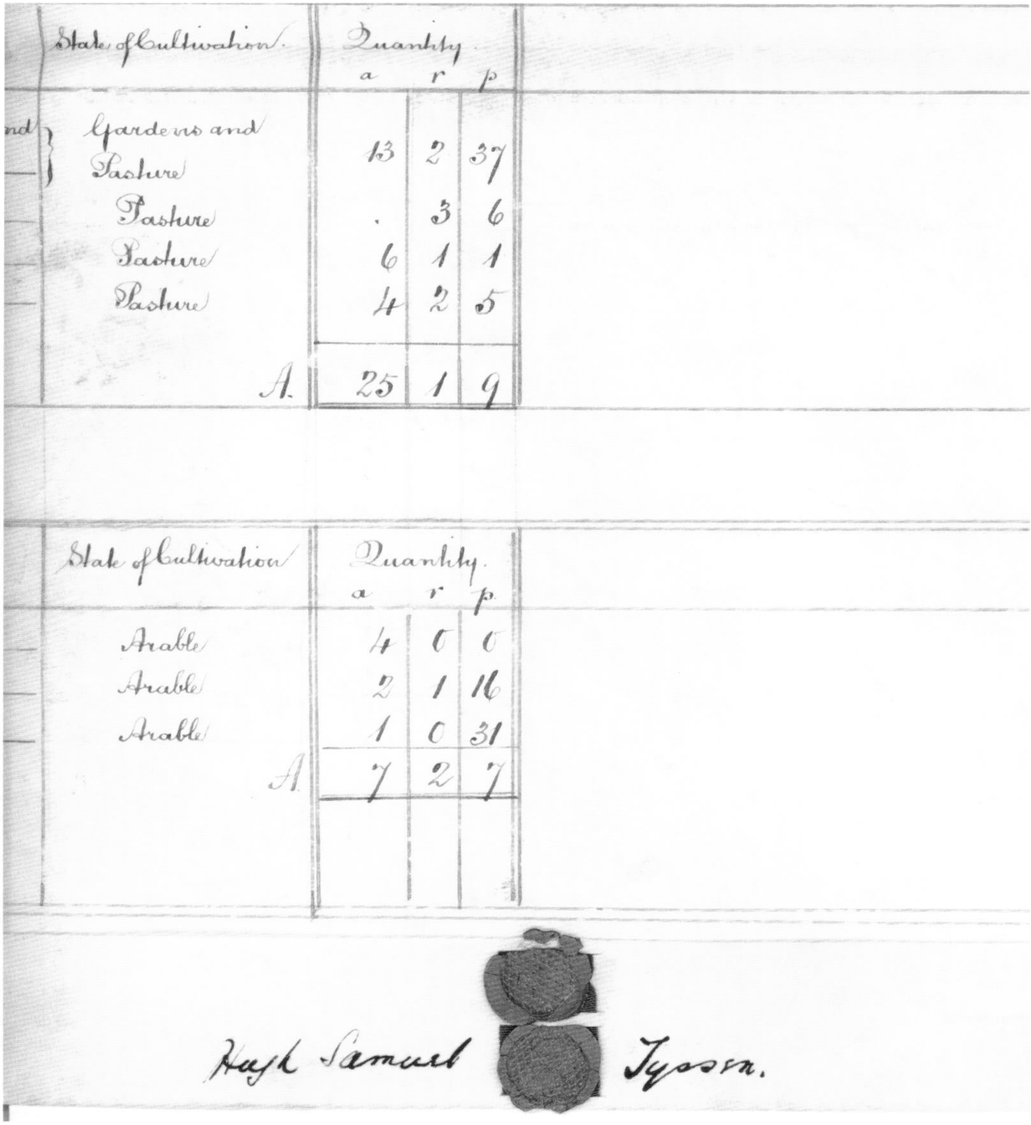

State of Cultivation	Quantity		
	a	r	p
Gardens and Pasture	13	2	37
Pasture	.	3	6
Pasture	6	1	1
Pasture	4	2	5
A.	25	1	9

State of Cultivation	Quantity		
	a	r	p
Arable	4	0	0
Arable	2	1	16
Arable	1	0	31
A	7	2	7

Hugh Samuel Tyssen.

20. Signature of Hugh Samuel Tyssen

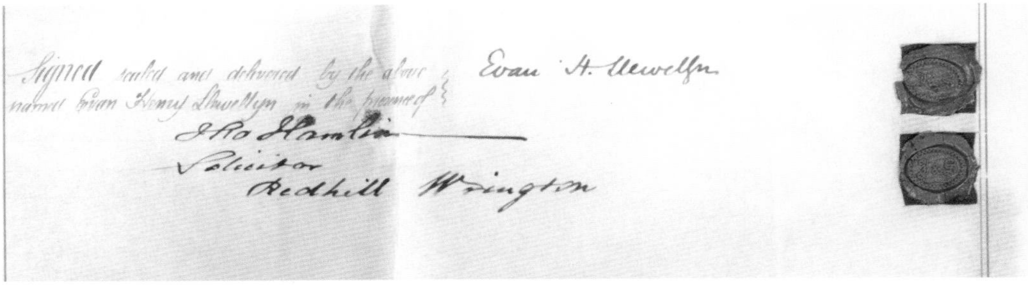

Signed sealed and delivered by the above named Evan Henry Llewellyn in the presence of Evan H. Llewellyn

J Ro Hamlin
Solicitor
Redhill Wrington

21. Signature of E. H. Llewellyn

22. Painting of The Langford Stores by Diana Cornish, 1978

23. Stone carving at Hopedale

24. Blackmoor Cottage before extension

25. Acacia House

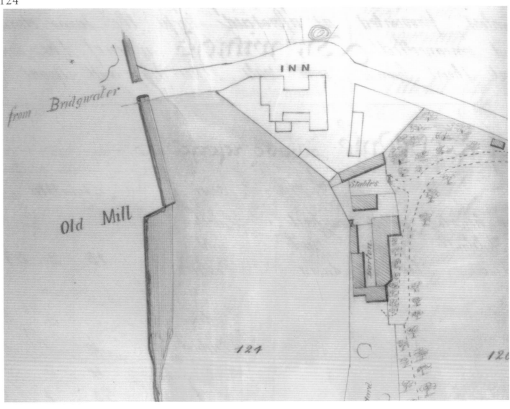

26. Estate map showing the Old Mill,

27. The Victoria Jubilee Homes

28. Painting of The Victoria Jubilee Homes

29. Statue of Queen Victoria outside The Victoria Jubilee Homes

30. Stone carving at The Victoria Jubilee Homes

31. Postcard of The Victoria Jubilee Homes

32. Maysmead Place

33. Oeil de Boeuf window at Maysmead Place

34. The west wing of Maysmead Place

35. The east wing of Maysmead Place

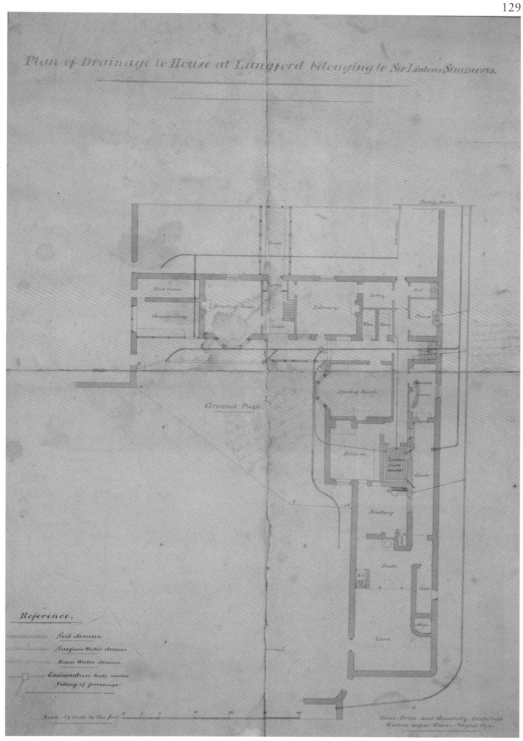

36. *Map of Somerlea including drainage plans, 1874*

37. Clock tower at Langford House

38. Postcard of Langford Court

-13-

1 Withey Cottages

Tristan Wilson

Numbers 1 and 2 Withey Cottages are a pair of semi-detached cottages about three quarters of the way along Blackmoor in the direction of Wrington. The name is derived from the "Withey Bed" that is noted on the site on the 1842 tithe map. The two cottages have been treated as one unit for some time, mostly with the owners living in No. 2, No. 1 then being rented to tenants. The two became separately owned in 1971.

The starting point for the history of Withey Cottages is the plaque on the front wall recording the cottages as having been built in 1893. The cottages were built by James Richards, originally a stone mason from Devon, who also built Star Cottage (between Withey Cottages and Blackmoor Cottage) and Chester House (on the corner of Greenwell Lane). By the time of the 1901 census, James had settled in Langford and was married to Harriet, with Herbert and Laura Berry as his step children.

Entry 83 in the 1901 census records William Legge, his wife Elizabeth and their four daughters and notes William's occupation as boot maker - he ran the eponymous "W. Legge and Son Hand-Sewn Boot and Shoe Makers" shop. Although this was attached to Star Cottage, where you can still see the outline of the shop roof, Star Cottage itself was owned and occupied by Miss Berry until the early 1980s. As the shop was at the end of the plot of land originally belonging to No. 1 Withey Cottages (the area now providing access to the garage belonging to No. 2) we can be confident that the Legges were living in No. 1.

The shoe shop diversified when, shortly after World War One, the post office moved into Legges from the house now known as "The Old Post Office" on the corner of Saxon Street. The photograph of Legge's shoe shop combined with Langford Post Office dates to 1923.

Photo of Legge's shoe shop

From here the Legges moved their business to Churchill, where they set up opposite what was then Cullen's, now Budgens, on a site that has most recently been the "Little Angels" nursery.

It is probable that the Legges were the first to occupy No. 1 Withey Cottages. The occupants of No. 2 on the 1901 census may have been the Baker family (George, Isabella and their three daughters and two sons), though this is not an adjacent plot number on the census (number eighty seven).

Judging by the dress of the subjects, the photo of Withey probably dates to around this period.

Photo of ladies at Withey Cottages

A family called Carpenter was living in No. 1 in about 1943, and may have been the tenants of the occupants of No. 2. 1950 saw Alexander Crane Johnson of No. 2 Withey Cottages selling both No. 1 and No. 2 to Arthur John Evans who, on his death in 1958, passed the cottages to his wife Lilian. The tenants at this point, or more certainly shortly after, were the Ellis family.

Mrs. Pat Fuller bought No. 1 from Lillian Evans in 1971, ending the period of joint ownership of the cottages. Modern facilities arrived shortly after in 1971/72 with the construction of an "...internal lavatory, fixed bath, wash hand basin and hot/cold water..." as recorded by Axbridge Rural District.

The next occupiers of No. 1 Withey Cottages were Karen and Tristan Wilson who moved in April 1997. Dillon Wilson was born to them in Southmead Hospital in 1997 and Frances was born in the front bedroom of No. 1 in 2001. In 2004 they moved, passing the care of No. 1 Withey Cottages to Mo and Andy Roberton, which brings the history up to date.

-14-

Laurel House

Jo Fryer

Laurel House is reputed to be the oldest house in Blackmoor and is believed to have been built in about 1700. It is thought that it was first sold in 1731 by William Adams to William Cross. The deeds show that it was sold again in1782 when John Cross signed with his 'mark'.

The deeds for Laurel House show that it was sold in 1731 by William Adams who is thought to have been the first owner of the property. The person who bought it was John Cross who was unable to sign his name and instead used his 'mark'.

Lloyds Bank Limited

TOTTERDOWN, Bristol.

SCHEDULE OF DEEDS, &c.

Owner's name in full   Austin Lovell

Property   Laurel House, Lower Langford, Churchill, Somerset.

Date	Description of Deed	Parties	
. 1732	Assignment	William Adams	William Cross
.1796	Release	William Cross	John Cross
t.1851	Lease	Lord Bishop of Bath & Wells	S. Parker
Feb.1852	Mortgage	S. Parker	J.P.Maine
. 187+	Assignment	S. Parker	J.P.Maine
. 1872	Conveyance	Ecclesiastical Commissioners	S. Maine & Crs.

Photocopy of extract from deeds

The mark of William Adams

The apportionment to the tithe map of 1842 shows the occupier to be Thomas Parker (senior). The property is described as house, shop and garden. No reference has been found as to what sort of shop it was.

The census return of 1841 confirms Thomas Parker (senior) aged 65 to be the occupier. He is listed as a farmer.

Name	Age	Occupation
Thomas Parker	65	Farmer
Louisa	25	
Elizabeth	25	
Samuel	20	

Census return 1841

In 1851 the census shows Thomas Parker to be the head of the household. It is presumed that he is the son of Thomas Parker senior as his age is recorded as 51. His father would have been 75 by now. Thomas Parker is recorded as a carpenter. The deeds show that S. Parker has a mortgage on Laurel House. S Parker is presumed to be Samuel, son of Thomas Parker.

Name	Age	Occupation
Samuel Parker	33	Carpenter
Sarah (wife)	31	
Charles Night	14	Servant

Census return 1851

It has not been possible to work out the names of the people living in Laurel House in 1861 and 1871.

The deeds show that Mr Maine sold the house to C D Loveless in 1888. Prior to this Charles D Loveless is shown on the census return for 1881 as head of household but has no occupation. The census states that he had been a telegraph worker. It is presumed he was leasing Laurel House from Mr Maine at this time.

Name	Age	Occupation
Charles D Loveless	40	No Occupation (was telegraph wire worker)
Jane (wife)	40	
John D (son)	16	Servant/coachman at Langford House
Frederick (son)	12	
Elisabeth (daughter)	10	
Dorcas (daughter)	8	
William (son)	5	
Agnes (daughter)	4	
Frank (son)	1	
Elizabeth	77	Mother, widow

Census return 1881

By the next census return in 1891, Charles D Loveless owned Laurel House and he is described as a taxidermist. His trade was to prepare, stuff and mount animal skins to give them a life-like appearance. It was popular in Victorian times to have animals or birds displayed in this way in glass cases. Charles D Loveless worked at home and used the downstairs room nearest the road as his shop and workroom.

Laurel House before the property was raised

Name	Age	Occupation
Charles D Loveless	50	Taxidermist
Jane (wife)	50	
Elisabeth (daughter)	20	Housemaid domestic service
Dorcas (daughter)	18	Nurse
William (son)	15	
Frank (son)	11	
Percy (son)	9	
Florence (daughter)	5	

Census return 1891

In 1890 the deeds show that the Lovelesses sold Laurel House to A. Ellet but bought it back again in 1893.

In 1901 Charles D Loveless is 60 years old and is still working as a taxidermist.

Name	Age	Occupation
Charles D Loveless	60	Taxidermist
Jane (wife)	60	
Dorcas (daughter)	28	
Frank (son)	21	Living on own means
Percy (son)	19	Horse keeper on farm
Florence (daughter)	15	Dressmaker

Census return 1901

The house looks as though it was built much later than the beginning of the 18th century on account of the major alterations it has had. In 1958 the house was bought by Austin Lovell who replaced the original windows with larger ones. At this time a well was found inside the house and the proximity to the Langford Brook made the house prone to flooding.

Note the roof on the right faces a different direction and the position of window by road is higher in relation to main house today

During the major floods of 1968 the house was seriously flooded. The owner, Austin Lovell, decided to raise the house by 5 feet 6 inches in order to prevent any recurrence of this. He planned and supervised the work himself and the house was rebuilt using the same external dimensions but the internal walls were moved to alter the size and shape of the rooms. Some of the original beams were incorporated into the new ceilings. Before the alterations you would step up to the room where the taxidermist used to work but after raising the rest of the house you now have to step down to it. The work was finished in 1972 and fortunately these drastic measures worked and the house was not flooded again.

The razing and raising of the house

After Austin Lovell died, his wife Phyllis died a short while after. The house was then sold to Jock and Jenny Renwick in 1996.

-15-

Hopedale

Liz Hyde

Hopedale is a detached stone-built Gentleman's Residence standing in approximately an acre of garden, which is bisected by the Langford Brook. Built in the Victorian era, it has seen various occupants in its relatively short history.

The earliest reference found to a property on the site is 1822. This is the date of a lease granted by the Ecclesiastical Commissioners for England to a John Masters. The lease appeared to be a life interest in the property and carried an annual rent of 6d. The site was described as 36 perches, (or 1089 square yards), somewhat smaller than it is today.

The 1841 census shows the Masters family occupying the cottage on the site. They consisted of John and Ann Masters and their three sons, John, Thomas and William. John senior is described as a shoemaker, as is his son, Thomas. John junior was a carpenter and William is described as an agricultural labourer.

By 1890, the property was only occupied by Thomas Masters. He would have been in the region of 70 years old. As he had a life interest in the property, he was party to a Conveyance, by which the Ecclesiastical Commissioners, represented by Richard, Lord Bishop of Bath & Wells, sold the property to a John Durban Loveless of Langford for the sum of £80. Mr Loveless is described as "a Coachman". The 1890 Conveyance does not give the cottage a name. It is simply identified by a plan.

John Durban Loveless

It is worth deviating a little at this point to delve into the provenance of Mr Loveless. The census return of 1881 shows the occupants of Laurel House, the house next door to the cottage, as being the Loveless family. These were listed as:-

> Charles D Loveless (40)
> Jane (wife) (40)
> John D (16) (described as groom/servant/coachman at Langford House)
> Frederick (12)
> Elisabeth (10)
> Dorcas (8)
> William (5)
> Agnes (4)
> Frank (1)
> Charles' mother, Elizabeth, also lived there (aged 77).
> She had originally come from Dunkeld in Scotland.

By the time of the next census in 1891, Charles was 50 and had become a taxidermist, and he and Jane had had two more children, Percy and Florence.

Perhaps young John was thinking of additional accommodation for his expanding brood of siblings for he was certainly quite the entrepreneur, having purchased Blackmoor Cottage (opposite the cottage) when he was only 22 for £50, and then the cottage three years later.

Although he purchased the house in 1890, he did not gain possession of it until the death of Thomas Masters in 1898. The year after, young John substantially improved the dwelling house and gave it the name of "Dunkeld", no doubt after his Grandmother's birthplace in Scotland. The current house has stone carving above the bay window denoting 1899 on one side of the bay and the initials JDL on the other side. It is not known whether any of the original cottage remains, or if it was demolished and the current house erected in its place.

Stone carving incorporating initials J. D. L.
(See Colour Plate 23, Page 122)

Stone carving incorporating date 1899

John Durban Loveless and family

In 1918, just after the end of the First World War, John Durban Loveless (now described as "Gentleman" in the Conveyance) sold both Dunkeld and Blackmoor Cottage to George Payne Warren, an accountant, for the combined sum of £750. The deeds indicate that Mr Warren had been in occupation of Dunkeld as tenant prior to buying it. The land was still 36 perches and only comprised land on the house side of the Langford Brook.

Later that year, (1918), Mr Loveless made a Statutory Declaration stating that he had made various building improvements to both properties, and that their descriptions in the Conveyances were correct in all respects. It is not known what necessitated this Declaration, but there was obviously some dispute or uncertainty that he was aiming to resolve.

John D Loveless went on to become Steward of Sydney Hill's Langford House Estate. In 1901, he and his wife, Amelia, were living at Langford House, where Amelia was housekeeper. It is believed that he later built Wyndhurst, where he was living in 1914.

During Mr Warren's six years of ownership, he must have changed the house's name, as, by the time it was sold at auction in 1924, it was called Hopedale. The purchaser was a medical practitioner called Alexander Hastings Whicher, of Clifton, Bristol. The purchase price was £1,100.

AT THE FOOT OF THE MENDIPS, LANGFORD,
SOMERSET.

CHARLES A. TRICKS & SON
are instructed by the Owner (who is leaving)
to SELL by AUCTION, at the GRAND HOTEL,
BROAD STREET, BRISTOL, on THURSDAY, the
3rd July, 1924, at Three o'clock in the Afternoon,
the Very Attractive Detached STONE-BUILT

VILLA   RESIDENCE,

known as

"HOPE DALE,"

Containing 3 Reception Rooms, Level Kitchen,
Ground Floor Cloakroom and w.c., Electric Light,
5 Bedrooms, Bathroom, and w.c. Good Garden.
Small Greenhouse. Water from a well. Together
with the FIVE-ROOMED COTTAGE and GARDEN
opposite, let at 5s weekly, tenant paying rates.
  If not sold in one lot the Properties will be
offered separately
POSSESSION OF RESIDENCE (but not Cottage)
on completion.

  Both Properties are Freehold and free from
Ground-rent, are near to the Post office, and
adjoin the 'Bus route.
  The Properties can be Viewed any day between
11 and 4 o'clock.
  For further particulars apply to the Auc-
tioneers, 18, St. Nicholas Street, Bristol; or to
Mr J. H. KING, Solicitor,
Edinburgh Chambers, 16, Baldwin Street,
Bristol.

1924 auction particulars front sheet

Twenty-two years later, in 1946, Dr Whicher sold Hopedale to Ella Catharine Bumsted of Ilminster for £4,000. Seven years later, Miss Bumsted died at Hopedale, and her executors sold the property in 1953 to Robert Chadwick Smith, a Bristol solicitor for the sum of £2,175.

The Smith family were instrumental in purchasing additional parcels of land. The field to the east of the house was purchased in 1957 and part of the current garden carved out of it. In 1964, Mrs Louie Monica Smith purchased part of the adjoining land from Acacia House, apparently so that she could create a duck pond!

Mrs Louie Monica Smith died in 1972 and Robert remarried in 1976. He had four teenage children, Peter, Tom, Louie and Kate, and Betty, his second wife, had three girls, Denise, Susan and Janet. Hopedale was clearly going to be quite squashed! Fortuitously, Blackmoor Cottage came on the market and the Smiths bought it as an annexe. The boys, Peter and Tom slept across the road at Blackmoor Cottage at night, and ate with the rest of the family at Hopedale.

By the time the current owners looked at the house in 1997 there was a land holding of around 10 acres, including the field to the east of the house. The vendor retained the field, although the enlarged garden means that the house is now set in just under one acre, somewhat more than the original 36 perches.

Alterations and improvements

Although the most major improvements were carried out by Mr Loveless, we do not know the precise extent of these. Nor do we know exactly which of the earlier owners carried out which works, but we do know that the Smith family erected the garage in 1958. As for the house, the auction particulars in 1924 refer to three reception rooms. We understand that, in approximately 1977, the front and back parlours were amalgamated to form one large drawing room. Before this, there was no room large enough in which the whole family could sit together!

The present owners, Richard and Elizabeth Hyde, and their two daughters, Alice and Rachel, in their nine years of ownership to date have made considerable changes to the house. These include:-

Staircase up to the attic rooms

Creation of a large family bathroom by sacrificing one of the bedrooms

Creating access from the playroom (formerly sitting room) to the kitchen

Enlarging the downstairs cloakroom to form a WC and shower room

Modernising the utility room and creating outdoor access therefrom

Large ground floor extension to the east of the kitchen to enlarge kitchen and create study/gym

The research into the history of a house is necessarily an ongoing process, and no doubt further information may emerge in the future.

-16-

Blackmoor Cottage

Jo Fryer

Blackmoor Cottage was built as a 2 up 2 down Victorian cottage in 1851 and was formerly known as 'The Cottage' until 1918 and Hopedale Cottage until 1968. It was inhabited by tenants until 1968 and since then has had owner occupiers. During the 2nd World War it was home to 6 evacuees from Bristol.

It is likely that there was an earlier cottage on the site of Blackmoor Cottage. It is shown on the apportionment of the tithe map of 1842 (plot 536) as a house and garden owned by William Paines and occupied by Richard Salter. After it was demolished the site would have been used for another cottage.

James Carter is shown on the churchwarden's accounts as the owner of the house and garden of 'The Cottage' at Blackmoor (plot 536) in 1851. In 1850 the plot is described as arable with no mention of a building and it may be assumed that Blackmoor Cottage, as it was later named, was built in 1851.

In 1851 James Carter was aged 46 and lived in Stock Lane with his wife Joanna 47 and his children Mary 18, Frederick 12, Celia 10 and Isaac 2. His occupation in the 1851 census is described as having a beer house. 'The Cottage' at Blackmoor would have been let to tenants.

Martha Hill is mentioned in the deeds as a previous tenant and in 1851 there is a record of the Hill family living in Blackmoor. John Hill as head of the house was 48 and an agricultural labourer. He lived with his wife Martha 49 and his children Elizabeth 22 a shoe binder, George 16 and William 13 both agricultural labourers and Ann 9 and Caroline 5 both scholars.

In 1881 Martha Hill appears on the census as a widow of 81 years living in Stock Lane with her unmarried daughter Caroline, 37 years. The property became void when John Hill died and Martha moved out. No reference has been found of the Carters living in Langford or Churchill in 1881, but in 1887 Joanna Carter's name appears on the deeds for 'The Cottage' when her heiresses agreed to sell the cottage or tenement at Blackmoor to Mr John D Loveless on the 3rd February 1887.

In the 1881 census J. D. Loveless was living at Laurel House (opposite) and was a servant, groom and coachman at Langford House. When he bought 'The Cottage' in 1887 he was 22 years old. On 16th June 1890 he also bought the house called across the road from 'The Cottage', called Dunkeld, made improvements to both properties and received rents from them. The property is described as a five roomed cottage and garden let at 6d yearly rent. J.D. Loveless later occupied Dunkeld himself.

In October 1918 J. D. Loveless sold Dunkeld and the 'cottage situate' in Blackmoor to Mr George Payne Warren for £750. George Warren changed the name Dunkeld to Hopedale and the cottage became known as Hopedale Cottage. In July 1924 he sold both properties by auction to Alexander Hastings Whicher for £1,000. The cottage is described as 'the piece or parcel of land on the tithe map number 536 and the messuage or dwelling house and premises formerly in the occupation of Martha Hill and then Mr Clark.' During this time William Roe and his wife Mabel rented the cottage.

Photo of Mabel

Mabel and Bill Roe lived here from the 1920s and had one child called Charlie. Bill cycled to work at the coal yard in Wrington and when Charlie was old enough he worked on Mr Owen's farm at Stepstones, a short walk up the road.

The living area of the cottage was to the right of the stairs (when viewed from the road) and it was here that the family spent most of their time. It had a range, which kept the room warm for most of the year. Under the stairs was a pantry, which had its own spring. During the time that Mabel and Bill lived here, they did not use the spring for their water supply, but often had to mop up when water seeped into the pantry. The room contained a table and chairs, at which most of the domestic tasks were done. Mabel had a budgie which she trained to talk and its cage was kept in this room. The budgie was able to distinguish who entered the room and would keep Mabel informed by saying, "There's Bill coming, Mabel," or "Here comes Charlie".

The downstairs room to the left of the front door was seldom used. It was kept as a best room and used at Christmas when the fire was lit. The rest of the time it always felt damp.

The kitchen was a single storey lean-to that had been built at the end of the building at the time the cottage was built. It was mostly used as a washroom and had a big deep stone sink and a cold water tap. A built in boiler was used for the family wash. An oil stove was used for cooking when the range was allowed to go out.

Picture of cottage before extension
(See Colour Plate 24, Page 123)

Like most cottages at this time there was no bathroom. A weekly bath would be taken in a zinc tub in front of the fire in the living room. An outside toilet and a 'coal house' were situated near the back door.

The garden was mainly used to grow vegetables for the family to eat. They also kept hens to provide them with eggs.

Upstairs in the cottage were two bedrooms, which gave the family plenty of space. But, during the Second World War, Hopedale Cottage became quite overcrowded, when Mabel's sister and children moved in as evacuees.

Mabel Roe's sister, Elsie Moss, was bombed out of Bristol in 1941 and came to Hopedale Cottage with five of her six children. Before joining the army Mr Moss was a lorry driver and he brought the family and their belongings to Langford in his vehicle. The number of people living in the '2 up 2 down' cottage suddenly increased from three to nine. The downstairs room, which had been the best room, was now used for sleeping as well as the two existing bedrooms. There were not enough beds for everyone and the children had to sleep on the floor.

Vegetables, especially potatoes, were grown in the garden and ration coupons were used in Ellesmore's Stores and the Post Office. Dennis, the oldest boy in Elsie's family can remember eating bread with butter that had been mixed with dripping to make it go further and having bread and jam for tea most evenings.

Mr Moss stayed in Bristol working with his lorry. Dennis was nine and as the oldest son, he stayed behind in Bristol to help look after his grandmother who did not want to be evacuated. After six months Dennis came to Hopedale cottage, having swapped with his next oldest brother who was called John, The very next day the house opposite where their gran lived was bombed and tragically both John and his grandmother were killed.

The children Dennis, Ron, Maureen, Ted and Sheila had each been issued with a gas mask in a square cardboard box, which they had to take to school every day. When they were in Bristol they had also been given a small tin of biscuits to keep with the gas mask in case they were hungry during an air raid. This was not needed in Langford and Churchill as they never needed to take their gas masks out of their boxes.

Dennis enjoyed living in the country and remembers 'scrumping' apples from the orchards belonging to Hopedale across the road. In the mornings before school he helped the local farmer milk the cows by hand. During the war years schools used to allow children in the villages twenty half days off school to help farmers. This was mainly in the summer. Dennis got up early every day to milk the cows and then spent the morning in school before working hard on the farm during the afternoon and evening. He would often find himself dropping off to sleep in lessons in school.

During the early years of the war Bill Roe's brother also lived at Hopedale Cottage. Jenny Roe, their spinster sister, lived by herself in one of the cottages at what is now Bay Tree Cottage. When the Moss family were evacuated from Bristol, Bill's brother moved across the road to create more space.

Jenny Roe was a regular attendee at the chapel and was buried there when she died in 1953 aged 85 years. Her grave can still be seen in the graveyard at the chapel.

Dennis can remember having to attend chapel every Sunday, not just once but three times! There was a service in the morning, Sunday School in the afternoon and another service in the evening. After a year Dennis and his family were able to move into one of a pair of condemned cottages (now Lockemore Cottage) just up the road and they lived there for the rest of the war. Shortly after the war was over the family were able to move into one of the new houses that the council built in Wrington.

Charlie Roe, as the only child of Mabel and Bill, must have keenly felt the presence of five Moss children, all under ten, moving into his small cottage. He was about ten years older than Dennis and initially did not have a lot to do with him and his brothers and sisters.

Photo of Charlie

By the end of the war Dennis was about thirteen and often went to the pub with Charlie. Despite being underage they took it in turns to buy a round. One evening when it was Dennis' turn to buy, he heard a voice behind him say "Hello Moss." He turned round and found himself facing his head teacher, Mr Williams. Not knowing how to handle the situation, Dennis asked him if he would like a beer, but Mr Williams declined. To Dennis' surprise and relief nothing was mentioned about the matter at school next day.

Alexander Whicher, the owner of Hopedale Cottage, was content to receive rent for the property and Mabel Roe continued to live there after she was widowed. On the 27th February 1967 the council declared the cottage unfit for human habitation under the housing act of 1957. It was not to be used for human habitation after Mrs Roe vacated it, until the council were satisfied that it had been rendered fit for the purpose. In November 1967, after Mabel Roe had died, building plans were submitted for the addition of a bathroom and on 6th December 1967 George Whicher sold Hopedale Cottage, still in its condemned state, to R C White (Builders) Ltd for £2,000. The building plans were passed in January 1968.

After adding a bathroom, R C White sold Hopedale Cottage on 29th March 1968 to Mrs Georgina Lillian Portass for £3,500, making a quick profit in less than four months.

The beginning of July 1968 was exceptionally hot with temperatures reaching 91 degrees. This culminated in terrific thunderstorms particularly in the west Mendip area. The Somerset River Authority estimated that 200 million tons of rain fell in 24 hours and in nearby areas such as Rowberrow, Shipham and Winscombe five inches of rain fell in just two hours. On July 14th it had rained for most of the day and water flowed off the saturated Mendips, filling the streams to bursting point. The Langford Brook became deeper and deeper. Unfortunately, this coincided with a high tide and the sluice gates at Kingston Seymour had been closed. Consequently, the water had nowhere to go and the brook burst its banks, flowed down the road and into all the properties at the side of the road. To make matters worse, a coach carrying people from the mushroom farm broke down on the downstream side of Hopedale Cottage creating a dam and causing the water to reach a depth of over five feet throughout Hopedale Cottage. A neighbour from the house across the road (Laurel House) decided to try to rescue the driver and passengers by placing a ladder from his garden wall into the doorway of the coach. A few brave souls clambered across to safety. The rest were stranded on the coach for several hours. People, travelling in a Mini, trying to get to Wrington suddenly found themselves swept up by the water and deposited on top of the hedge belonging to Hopedale Cottage.

When the tide went out and the sluice gates were opened, the water receded rapidly leaving sludge over furniture and furnishings as well as badly stained walls. Much of the furniture and many of the belongings were ruined, but fortunately the weather was hot and sunny for the next three weeks for the drying out and cleaning up operation to begin.

The flooding experience put Mrs Portass off living in Langford and at the first opportunity she sold Hopedale Cottage to Brian Fisher in December 1968 for £4,200, having lived there for just eight months.

Mr Fisher changed the name to Blackmoor Cottage and added a garage. He lived in Blackmoor Cottage for three and a half years before selling to Peter Cobbs for £9,000.

Peter Cobbs lived in the cottage for four years before selling to David and Annie Scotland for £10,500. They had three boys whose increasing heights were measured on the kitchen wall. Annie was 'artistic' and painted a full size Friesian cow on the kitchen wall. The walls of the dining room were painted a bright mustard colour while the fireplace was also mustard but with red grouting and a green, wooden surround.

In April 1976 the Scotlands sold Blackmoor Cottage for £13,500 to Robert Smith, who lived across the road at Hopedale. He had remarried and he and his wife Betty had seven teenage children between them. The older sons used Blackmoor Cottage as an annex to Hopedale, eating at Hopedale by day and sleeping at Blackmoor Cottage by night. As some of the children started to leave home, Bob and Betty Smith sold the cottage to Jo and Mike Fryer in 1978 for £18,000.

The Fryers have lived in Blackmoor Cottage for 28 years. In their time the cottage has been extended to four bedrooms and the overall size has been increased by 60%.

-17-

Devonshire House

Mary Barnfield

Research has thrown up very little about Devonshire House. Sadly the deeds have been lost and there are large gaps in its history. The construction, with thick rubble stone internal walls, may suggest the current house was built on the site of an existing smaller building, but there is no other evidence to support this.

Devonshire House was built during the early 1800s. The outside walls are a good 40cm (16in) thick and made of rubble stone. However there is also an internal wall running across the house which does suggest that the front may have been added at a slightly later date. There is evidence in the loft that the roof has been raised at some time but this is not unusual. The sash windows in the front have been replaced with leaded windows.

There is an original pantry which was probably outside the house but has since been incorporated into the kitchen. There is also a single story side extension, the front of which is part of the house and the back used as a store room; the date of this is unknown. It is difficult to define Devonshire House, is it a large cottage or a small house?

The 1842 tithe apportionment tells us that Joseph Wood owned the house and land of 1 acre, 1 rood and 13 perches and that James Kingcott (30), a farmer and his wife Elizabeth (30) lived there with their four young children: Mary (5), James (3), Sarah (2) and Alfred (4 months). Also living in the house were three children of "independent means", going by the name of Haskins: Elizabeth (15), Sarah (15) and Henry (10). These were Elizabeth's children from her first marriage. Although James rented the house, he owned land around Langford and is referred to as a farmer rather than an agricultural worker or labourer which indicates that he had a reasonable income. By 1851 it would appear that the Kingcott family had returned to Lodge Farm, prior to emigrating to Australia (see Chapter 5).

We now have to move on a few years to 1871 when we believe that John Chapman, then aged 71, his wife Hannah aged 66 and one of their sons, Joseph, lived there. He is referred to as a "retired dissenting minister", however in an earlier census he is a Baptist minister. Originally from Devon, he had married Hannah who came from Banwell and his sons were born in Stogumber, in Somerset. As a retired minister he would have been a respected member of the community and would have had a good income. John Chapman is buried in the Evangelical Church graveyard in Blackmoor, and so probably worshipped there. Hannah continued to live in the house and was still there in her seventy sixth year. A little research revealed that Joseph became an accountant and moved to Bedminster, where his mother joined him and was living with his family in 1891 aged eighty six.

There is a photograph of Devonshire House taken during the 1880s when it was known as South View. We have yet to discover who the lady sitting on the seat in front of the house is.

Postcard of lady in front of Devonshire House

In 1978 an elderly lady from Australia visited the house and spoke to the owner. She recalled living there in 1913 and the family providing cream teas for charabanc parties who travelled out to the country from Bristol. During the 1920s and 1930s the property was used as a market garden and at one time run by a family called Elton.

In about 1943 two retired teachers from London called the Misses Devonshire bought "South View" and changed its name to Devonshire. They also planted fir trees all around the house. After the Second World War they gave (or sold) the house to a national teachers' union, but built a bungalow for themselves at one end of the garden. Devonshire House was also used as a convalescent home. During this time wood block floors were laid in the three reception rooms; these remain today. I imagine this is also when some of the windows were replaced with rather ugly metal window frames and possibly the layout of the bedrooms was altered. The house had a full time housekeeper and gardener. In the late 1950s a Miss Crossman was housekeeper but the house was by then a home for retired teachers.

During the 1960s the house reverted back to a family home and was owned by Trevor Jones, the Somerset cricketer. In 1976 it changed hands again and a detached garage block with a studio over was built in the 1980s. Also at this time another house was built in part of the garden. The new house and the 1940s bungalow are no longer part of Devonshire House.

Devonshire House remains today as a family home in a beautiful garden and will no doubt continue to evolve as it has done over the last two centuries.

Gravestone of John Chapman and Hannah Chapman

Postcard of Devonshire House in the 1940s

-18-

Acacia House

Mike Fryer

It is not known exactly when the house was built or when it was given the name Acacia House. However, the site is identified on the 1842 Churchill Parish tithe map (ref 534) with a building identified and the 1841 census correlates with this confirming that a family was living at a property with this reference. This would suggest that a property has existed on the site for at least 165 years. As well as being a dwelling house it is known to have been used as a funeral parlour and possibly at different times as a sawmill, Post Office and a kindergarten, although not verified.

Acacia House is located in Blackmoor. The front of the cottage faces southwards towards the Mendip Hills. To the front elevation there is an open porch that leads onto a small cottage garden. There is an Acacia tree in the garden which may have been where the name of the cottage was derived. To the rear there is a small yard and outbuildings. The cottage is sited immediately adjacent to the Langford Brook to the east and its west gable end wall bounds the lane that runs from Langford to Wrington.

It is a two storey building generally constructed in a cottage style. The external walls are built in stone with a cement render finish. Notable features of the property include a low sloping roof at the rear and the gable end walls that extend above the roof line to form a sloping parapet capped with stone coping stones. Between the parapets is a pitched roof covered with clay pantiles

The porch to the front elevation is brick construction with glazed windows each side topped out with a pitched slate roof. This construction contrasts with the style of the rest of the property and suggests it may be either a later addition or has been rebuilt at some time.

Internally, the property has low ceilings, but has no other significant features maintaining an air of functionality which include stone flag floors beneath the carpet coverings. The present owner says it is rumoured that a donkey may be buried beneath the flags, but no evidence exists of this and there are no reported sightings of any ghostly braying, long eared quadrupeds to give this rumour the credence it might deserve.

Its proximity to the Langford Brook begs the question as to whether during its life it might have utilised the flowing water source for power or some other small industrial purpose such as in connection with the tanning and leather related works that have prevailed in the area historically. There is however now no evidence to support this possibility and the shallow slow flowing stream that we see today does not give much credence to this theory, but it is said that the brook was once much deeper and fast flowing with a good stock of trout that the locals fished using lines and by tickling.

Returning to the earliest documentary records namely the 1841 Census and 1842 tithe map, these show that the cottage was owned and occupied by a carpenter Thomas Parker aged 40, his wife Sarah 39, and what can reasonably be assumed to be their three children, Mary aged 10, John 5 and Thomas 9 months.

The census of 1851 confirms the Parker family were still in Blackmoor, assumed to be at Acacia House, but suggests that a tragedy may have befallen the family inasmuch that the youngest member Thomas, was not with them anymore and it is probably reasonable to assume this was a child death. However the Parkers appear not to have been deterred by this and a new name Sarah aged 8 appears on this census who would have been conceived a little over one year after the 1841 census.

The 1861 census records the Parker family still living in Blackmoor, including all three children Mary now age 30 John 25 and Sarah 18. Mary is recorded as being a dressmaker and John appears to have followed in his fathers footsteps as a carpenter.

By the time of the 1871 census, the Parker family are no longer a unit living in Blackmoor and the records show that only the youngest family member, daughter Sarah appears to be living in Blackmoor but on her own. Her name also appears in the 1881 census as being resident in Blackmoor and her occupation at this time is recorded as being a governess.

The occupations of the two Parker daughters, Mary and Sarah respectively recorded as dressmaker and governess, would not be typical in most country villages but quite likely result from demand from the unusually high proportion of local gentry that lived in the larger houses roundabout.

It appears that brother John had not moved far as there is record on the 1871 Burrington Census of a John Parker carpenter age 36, and if the same is now married to Ann Parker 38 and living in a grocer shop in Lower Langford. They both are still recorded as residents in Lower Langford in 1881 as Carpenter and shopkeeper respectively.

John and Ann Parker appear again in the 1891 Census, but John is now also recorded as Post Master of the Old Post Office on Langford Road. Living with them are Sarah his sister and a nephew Thomas Roberts who is recorded as a Post Office Assistant and as being born in Kidderminster.

So, it appears that by 1891 any direct Parker family links with Acacia house had come to an end. It is not evident from the 1891 or 1901 census whether Acacia House was occupied and the trail goes cold for a while. However the present occupant believes that the house may have been owned by a Mr Jimmy Tucker in the 1930s.

It is said that Jimmy Tucker may have operated a small sawmill at the property and the current occupant believes there is still evidence of the equipment to be found in the yard area that may have been used in this connection. If this is the case, it again begs the question raised earlier as to whether the proximity of the Langford Brook may have been used in connection with the sawmill. Jimmy is believed to have been the owner of the donkey that is allegedly buried beneath the floor in the cottage.

It has not been possible to establish any information about Jimmy Tucker, but it is possible that he may have been a landlord and owner of Acacia House for a time but was not a resident in the area.

The present occupant Polly King believes that the house was purchased by her uncle, Mr Gilbert Roberts for around £500 from Jimmy Tucker probably during the 1930s.

Gilbert George Roberts is believed to have been born in Upper Langford at Grange Farm around 1896. The 1901 Census lists a Gilbert Roberts age 5 as son of Thomas and Kate Roberts, Thomas being a carpenter and born in Kidderminster, Worcestershire.

This appears to be the same Thomas Roberts, post office assistant in 1891 at the Old Post Office on the Langford Road run by his uncle John Parker who had previously lived at Acacia house between 1841 and 1871.

Gilbert was a longstanding resident in the parish of Churchill and except for the period he served during the 1914 -1918 war, lived in the area all of his life. It is said that he may have lived in Bay Cottage in Blackmoor before moving into Acacia House in 1942 prior to which he had let Acacia House. He was married to Mabel Roberts but they did not have any descendants.

It is said that Gilbert retained youthful appearance that belied his age and that he was also a man of large stature and strong voice and made his presence felt whenever in the company of others.

As a boy Gilbert was a chorister at St Mary's Langford, and later became a member of the Churchill choir for some 50 years until his death. He was also a senior member of the Parochial Church Council and it is also said that he was an active supporter of the British Legion Benevolent Fund and won a gold medal for services rendered. It appears that Gilbert like his father was a carpenter and decorator. These skills were it seems extended into coffin making and he was also the local undertaker and Acacia House was used as funeral parlour during this time. He was clearly very active in the local community also finding time to play cricket for the Langford Cricket team.

Gilbert and Mabel were Polly King's aunt and uncle and lived together in Acacia House until Mabel died in 1958. Following Mabel's death Polly moved into Acacia House to look after her uncle Gilbert until November 1962 when at the age of sixty seven he met an untimely death when he stepped off a bus at Churchill into the path of a passing car and was killed.

Polly King still lives in the property and has commented that she believes the house may also have been used as a Post Office and also a kindergarten at some time, but it has not been possible to verify this.

-19-

The Hall

Jo Fryer

In its time 'The Hall' has been a mill, a drill hall for the Light Infantry, a village hall, a police station as well as a private home.

It is unknown when the terraced property behind the present Post Office was built but it was definitely once the home of a miller. It is known that when the tannery, situated on the opposite side of the road, was for sale, it was advertised in the *Bristol Mirror* of 15th June 1811. The description of the premises for sale included a mill-house.

The tithe map of 1842 identifies the property as tithe number 659 and describes it as a mill and land. The apportionment shows the owner to be William Isley who also owned the adjacent plots numbers 660 and 661 which are described as outer orchard and orchard and stable. The occupier or tenant at this time was Richard Bacon. This is confirmed by the census of 1841 when Richard Bacon appears as a miller, age 45 with a wife Jane, 30 and children John 7, Elizabeth 5, Fanny 1 and Harriett 12 months.

The 1851 census return shows John Bell to be a master miller in this area, but in 1861 it has not been possible to identify who was living at the mill then or if indeed it was still used as a mill.

Various old maps feature the position of the sluice gate and it is possible to see the remains of its thereabouts in the brook next to the property that housed the mill.

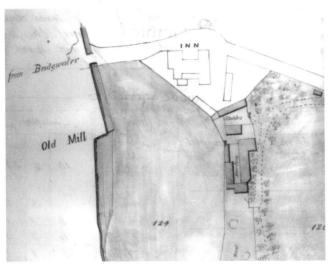

Old estate map showing mill, 1884
(See Colour Plate 26, Page 124)

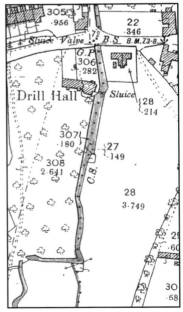

OS Map showing sluice gate

It is known that the property nearest the brook was once used as accommodation by the Light Infantry for at least thirty years in the second half of the 19th century and also in the early 20th century. The house is now called The Hall. The property at the other end of the building was the Drill Hall and as such had no ceilings. The roof space was exposed plaster and lath.

The census returns tell us that in 1871 a V. Woodbridge, age 31, a captain unattached in the Light Infantry, was living on the premises with his wife Jane, age 27. Jane was born in the Cape of Good Hope and their son James W. was born there. Their next three sons, ? 5, William 3 and Herbert 1 were born in the East Indies.

By 1881 William Fletcher, age 46, was living at the Drill Hall with his wife Marion, age 31 and their five daughters Helen 14, Mary 12, Elisabeth 9, Marion 7 and Blanche 9 months. William is described as a sergeant instructor of volunteers. He and his wife were born in Scotland as were the three oldest girls. The younger two were born locally.

From the census returns of 1871 and 1881 we can see that the army personnel living at the Drill Hall were not local people as was also the case in 1891, when the head of the household had been born in Ireland. He was Thomas Morissey, age 41 and described as an ex-sergeant of the Somerset Light Infantry. His wife was Ellen, age 37 and they had three children Thomas 5, Hilda 3 and Nora 1.

At the turn of the century there had been another change and Fred Abbott, age 38, was a sergeant for Somersetshire Light Infantry. He had been born in Somerset and was married to Susan, age 26. Their children were Agnes 5, George 3 and Elizabeth 1.

It is not known how frequently the army residents moved on and it is quite likely that there were other army people occupying the house between the dates of the census returns

The village benefited from the army presence as concerts were arranged from time to time. In April 1891 the Churchill Parish magazine advertised the annual concert to be held at the Drill Hall.

No. 16.   PRICE 1d.

Churchill Parish Magazine.

APRIL, 1891.

"Watch ye, stand fast in the faith."

SPECIAL · NOTICE FOR THIS MONTH:

TUESDAY, APRIL 21st,

ANNUAL CONCERT

AT THE

DRILL HALL, LANGFORD,

AT 7.30 P.M.

WESTON-SUPER-MARE:
W. SPENCER, PRINTER, ETC., ST. JAMES' STREET.

Advertisement from the Churchill Parish magazine

The Third Voluntary Battalion Somerset Light Infantry, to give them their full title disbanded and the Drill Hall was used as a village hall where dances were held. This is the closest Langford has been to having its own village hall but imagine the health and safety issues today if it was known that the army rifles were stored in the room above!

At some stage the Volunteer Battalion became known as the Territorials and a local man, John cook, was used for the recruiting posters. At seven feet four inches tall he was the tallest man in the army.

The army volunteers must have disbanded round about 1911 as the whole building was put up for sale in 1911 when it was described as 'a milling premises with a powerful stream running by thereby… and which may be easily converted for factory purposes, but now used as a Drill Hall for the 3rd Voluntary Battalion Somerset L.I. and a five roomed cottage, gardens and premises.'

It is known that there had been a mill here prior to the Light Infantry using The Hall. Maybe the description was subject to a little bit of Estate Agent's 'blurb' as I do not think anyone would describe the brook as 'a powerful stream running by' today. It did not sell as a mill or a factory and it was still vacant during the First World War when it was used as a Police Station. It was later converted to living accommodation and today the building is divided into three properties providing homes for three families.

The Hall converted to multiple dwellings

Prior to 1927 and possibly from around the time the property was sold after the First World War, after its use by the Light Infantry, Mabel and Edgar Day lived in The Hall and ran a confectioners and newsagents. They also had a tea garden behind the shop. They lived here until just after the Second World War and Mr. and Mrs. English moved in, but they did not run a shop. The next people to live at The Hall were Mrs. Phillips and her son and daughter. Mrs. Phillips ran the post office which moved to here in 1940.

Mr and Mrs Small were the next people to live at The Hall. They ran the Post Office and also introduced a grocery shop. They also owned the property attached to theirs and rented it to the Tincknell family for many years. They lived at The Hall for thirty-five years and when they retired, they sold the Post Office as a separate business. The two residential properties were sold in one transaction to Myra and Dave Ellis who turned them into one house.

Myra and Dave Ellis lived in The Hall from 1990 until 2006. When they were having the foundations laid for an extension, they did not hit solid ground until they reached 8 to 10 feet down on the side nearest the brook. The ground had been filled in with all sorts of rubbish in order to block up the diversion of the brook that had once been created for the water wheel. They were able to identify the point at which the water wheel was fixed to the wall as some of the fittings were still visible at the side of the house. The brook has remnants of where a sluice gate was fitted to divert the water to the wheel.

An old flint lock rifle was also found when digging for the foundations for the extension. It was in a bad state but was obviously a relic from the times the Light Infantry were at The Hall.

-20-

The Victoria Jubilee Homes

Joy Morris

This imposing red brick Victorian building, surrounded by gardens and shrubbery, always catches the eye of anyone visiting the village for the first time. Often mistaken for a nursing home, it is in fact a terrace of six fine almshouses.

Built during the last decade of the Victorian era to a very high standard, presumably by local craftsmen, the Homes were commissioned and endowed in 1891 by Simon Sidney Hill of Langford House.

"In commemoration of the Jubilee of the Ascension of Her Gracious Majesty Queen Victoria to the throne of Great Britain and Ireland".

He most generously bequeathed these buildings to be used for housing for *"those who are in advanced years, are in straightened circumstances and without near relatives who in the opinion of the Trustees could be considered in a position to help them, and also are of connection with the Founder's family"*.

The founding deed stated that the private income of any occupant is not to exceed £50 per annum, but authorises a supplementary allowance from the Trust of £30 per annum for each household.

Although not stated in the deeds, which were adopted by the Board of Trustees, minutes of the meeting prefix the qualifications for suitable residents with the description *'gentlefolk'*!

In order to create this act of generosity, land was acquired which was stated as being an orchard, house, six cottages, and a tanyard bordering the turnpike road leading from Bristol to Exeter.

Recent research has found that while the house on the site was uninhabited and semi-derelict, the row of cottages, known as Granger's Row or The Row, housed as many as twenty-three people.

Early painting of Jubilee Homes 1890s
(See Colour Plate 28, Page 125)

In 1888 and 1889 the site was cleared ready for the building of the Homes. Rookery Farm with its 65 acres of farmland as well as another 22 acres of land known as "Smallways", both in Congresbury, were also purchased as an endowment for provision of income to maintain the Homes. In 1899 a further £1,000 was donated to this fund.

The original deeds specified that residents must be members of a Protestant Christian Church, Roman Catholics and Unitarians were specifically excluded. Records from 1907 show that there was an attempt to have this rule amended legally. However, it was confirmed by Counsel that this could not be altered. It was also the intention that all of the six houses should be lived in by more than one person and single occupancy was discouraged.

After the death of Simon Sidney Hill and four years after the death of his nephew who had succeeded him, Thomas Sidney Hill, his great nephew took over as Chairman of the Trust. Since that time various other locals have been nominated to the board of Trustees including, up until this day, many direct descendants of the Hill family. The present Chairman of the Board is Mr.J.C.B.Hunt, a grandson of Thomas Sidney Hill.

Lots of additions have been made to the houses throughout the last century. In 1924 electricity was installed and the supply was provided by The Winscombe Electric Light and Power Company. A note in the records states that it would have come at least two years earlier if the Company could have accepted additional consumers. The internal supply of fresh water was in 1947 supplemented by a mains service. The remains of a large pump stand in the present garden which was presumably used until the connection of mains supply.

In 1958 the Trustees were able to realise their ambition for comprehensive modernisation of the Homes when the Trust became a member of the National Association of Almshouses. This was completed in 1961 when bathrooms were installed as well as a hot water supply. It was not until 1970 that central heating was installed. Even more surprising was that the occupants were not asked to make a residential contribution until 1972. Since that time there have been annual increases and now a contribution is made which is comparable with modern rented accommodation.

Interior decoration is the responsibility of the residents but with certain strict rules that none of the woodwork or stone fabric of the building should be painted. No structural or other alterations can be made, as in 1987 the building was confirmed as a Grade II listed building, which forbids the alteration of the exterior and interior, and requires permission for even the most minor changes.

In later years, when it has been necessary to have skilled craftsmen to renovate or replace both stonework and the extensive wood fascias, the workmen always come down from the scaffolding amazed at the skill and workmanship of the original builders.

Statue of Queen Victoria
(See Colour Plate 29, Page 125)

During recent years it was a tradition to celebrate the birthday of a resident by the whole community gathering for a tea party under the huge redwood trees in the large communal garden which is at the end of the site.

Verbal history confirms that the majority of the people, who have lived in the houses over the years, have been very happy and there has always been great comradeship amongst them. There is always great amusement over the original rules which state among other things, *"no dogs, fowls, pigeons, pigs or other animal (except a cat) shall be kept at or in the Homes!"*

If the tenants needed reminding of their good fortune, every house had a large framed photograph of their benefactor, Simon Sidney Hill.

-21-

Maysmead Place

Michael Phillips and Emma Phillips

Originally an agricultural dwelling with a few acres of land, Maysmead Place became a 'Regency Cottage Ornée' or small gentrified house, when it was extended using features from the Gothic revival of the second half of the 18th century. It was finally enlarged in the early 1900s to become the large country house it is today.

Introduction

This is an account of a building which, over a period of more than two hundred years, has gone through a metamorphosis from a humble agricultural dwelling to a country house. It is an example of how a building can progressively be altered and adapted to suit the changing needs of successive owners without destroying its character. At a time when many homeowners are pre-occupied with "makeovers" of their homes and gardens, it is worth remembering that this is not a recent trend. Major alterations and extensions tend to take place during times of prosperity and it is a fact that historic buildings survive best when money is short and owners are reluctant to tinker with them. The later Georgians substantially altered the appearance of older buildings by changing the fenestration to sash windows, a practice not so far removed from the present day replacement of original windows with UPVC double glazing, and the Victorians spoilt many old properties by adding extensions which were out of harmony with the style and proportions of the original building.

The Cottage Ornée

As the eighteenth century progressed there was a great expansion of interest amongst the leisured classes in what was described as the Picturesque. Hitherto, nobody had shown much interest in the dramatic scenery of the highlands of Scotland or North Wales but many returning from a Grand Tour of Europe, and particularly from Italy, and influenced by the classical landscape paintings of Poussin and Claude Lorraine, started to explore the wilder parts of their own country and developed a taste for scenery. This led to a demand for the naturalistic landscape garden on their estates, so famously designed by Lancelot "Capability" Brown and later by Humphrey Repton, scattered with classical pavilions and statuary copied from Italian originals.

At the same time there was a reaction to the classic Palladian style, which had originated in Italy and dominated the design of domestic architecture in England for one hundred and fifty years and imposed strict rules of proportion, symmetry, austerity of decoration and formality. A movement began in the second half of the 18th century towards the more ornate, Gothic style, much used since the Middle Ages in ecclesiastical architecture. A well known exponent of this style was Horace Walpole, who built an elaborate and highly decorated house overlooking the Thames at Twickenham called Strawberry Hill which was subsequently much imitated. This was to pre-date by a hundred years the Victorian obsession with Gothic revival as in Pugin's Houses of Parliament. Meanwhile, at the turn of the 18th/19th Centuries it became fashionable for the land-owning classes to ornament their parks by rebuilding their workers' cottages in a rustic style (e.g. Blaise Castle Estate, Bristol). Hitherto the question of the upper classes living in a cottage, however large, was unthinkable but new cottages of considerable size were now built as seaside villas or hunting lodges (e.g. Knowle Cottage, Sidmouth and Endsleigh Cottage near Tavistock. The final seal of approval was the building by the Prince Regent in 1812 of a large Cottage Ornée known as Royal Lodge in Windsor Great Park.

The rising middle classes, rapidly becoming more numerous and more prosperous in Regency times, were not slow to follow this trend and Cottages Ornées were built in many rural and seaside locations in the West Country and elsewhere, sometimes as permanent residences. Mendip Lodge at Upper Langford was a grander example of the elaborate Regency Gothick style, built by Dr. Whalley, a clergyman from Bath, as a summer residence and now demolished. He was a friend of the Ladies of Llangollen in North Wales, who, as young women eloping from Ireland, settled in a cottage in Llangollen, in which they spent the rest of their lives ornamenting and improving. Such was their fame for originality of decorative styles that they were visited by many of the members of Regency society from the Queen and the Duke of Wellington downwards. They refer in their Journal to Dr. Whalley being "on his Mendip Mountain". It has been suggested that the gothic windows in Mendip Lodge and those at Maysmead Place were probably made by the same local craftsmen.

Cottage Ornée would appear to be a French name but it seems that it is another fanciful English invention as was Gothick, which could mean anything from a few Georgian French windows with thin glazing bars and pointed arches, as in the case of Maysmead Place, to a stone faced building with mullion windows and church style decoration.

Origins

Maysmead Place is considered to be a good example of a Regency Cottage Ornée, but it is not entirely what it appears. Unlike the classic Georgian houses in the village designed and built for the "Gentry", it grew over a long period into an eclectic mix of styles. It is situated at the end of the metalled section of what is now called Maysmead Lane about a quarter of a mile north of the centre of Lower Langford village. Although the name Maysmead has romantic connotations of summer pasture land in the same way as the ancient meaning of the name of Somerset is the land of summer grazing, sadly, we have been unable to find any justification for such origins. We know that the name of the house was changed in 1912 from Langford Cottage and that on the 1903 OS map another name, of Blackmoor Lodge, was used, no doubt reflecting its proximity to the hamlet of Blackmoor at a time when its land bordered the Wrington road. Maysmead Lane was originally called Redshard Lane, which name has, since the 1950s, applied only to the un-metalled section leading from Stock Lane. The 1883 OS map shows it as Redshord Lane. It has been suggested that the name relates to red shards (i.e. fragments of pottery, possibly Roman) being found in the vicinity. However, the Oxford English Dictionary gives alternative meanings of a shard or sherd as 1. a gap in an enclosure esp. in a hedge or bank or 2. a patch of cow dung. Either seems possible! A long term resident of the village tells us that until the local authority erected street names it was known as

Taylor's Lane after the name of the owners of Maysmead in the inter-war years!

The earliest part of the house now forms the west wing and is believed to date from the second half of the seventeenth century. It is three storeys high with low ceilings on the ground floor. We have discovered traces of a staircase which rose from what is now the kitchen to a landing on the first floor. On the east side was an open courtyard with a well, now covered over, which provided pumped water to the house until the installation of mains water in 1954. This was reached through an arched porch, traces of which can still be seen. In the south east corner looking in to what currently is the pantry but once was an outside wall, there remains a "squint" or narrow tapering aperture which at one time apparently afforded some ventilation to what was then a dairy. On the first floor was a single long room and a narrow winding staircase led to the second storey consisting of two attic rooms. All the windows on the first and second floors of this part of the house have been changed in subsequent years to sash windows on the first floor and casements on the second, and a parapet wall runs the length of the west wing.

The west wing
(See Colour Plate 34, Page 128)

The present owners discovered some twenty eight years ago the foundations of a building in the north-west corner of the garden adjoining Redshard Lane. Near this was a perfectly preserved well hidden under a stone slab which was buried under a foot of soil. The 1883 OS map and Tithe map of this period show this to have been the site of a small dwelling and yard which had disappeared from the 1903 edition of the map.

Gentrification

By the turn of the 18th to 19th Centuries, people of "the middling sort", the more successful tradespeople of Bristol and the professional men who ministered to their needs, were growing in numbers and prosperity. At the same time Bristol city centre was becoming a very unpleasant place in which to live, hence the migration up the hill to Clifton of those with the necessary means. However, some preferred to establish country residences or villas, as they were then rather fancifully called, and Lower Langford, on the Bristol to Exeter coach road and only 12 miles from Bristol City centre (two to three hours by horse or carriage) seems to have attracted a disproportionate number of new residents, as witnessed by the relatively large number of sizeable houses of that period. In addition, some residents of Bath (e.g. the clergyman, Dr. Whalley) found that Bath, out of season in the summer, was unpleasantly close and established a summer residence in the area. Thus a nucleus of local "Society" was formed which in turn attracted further incomers. When one remembers that a tannery was situated where the Methodist Homes now are and which must have emitted the most nauseating stench it is surprising that the owners of sensitive nostrils could tolerate it!

It was at this time that "Langford Cottage" was extended, again with rubble stone, rendered and colour washed, and transformed into a residence suitable for the "Gentry" in the style of the then fashionable Cottage Ornée. The main, or south facing, portion of the house was either added or substantially altered in 1811, according to a date carved in the rafters. There is some evidence that the original roof was probably thatched, and that the roof pitch was altered when it was subsequently slated. At the same time the ceiling height on the ground floor was altered to allow the correct Georgian proportions for the downstairs rooms then consisting of a parlour and another sitting room, probably also used as a dining room as was the practice at that time, and arranged symmetrically on either side of the entrance hall which gave access to the original kitchen at the rear in the earlier part of the house. The doors, skirtings, architraves, staircase and mouldings are clearly of the Regency period as are the classic French windows (opening inwards) and first-floor windows although the latter have subsequently been converted to casements from sashes, which proved impractical with the gothic pointed shape. The fireplaces are of later origin. The stairs led to a sub-landing with a gothic window looking north and access on the right to a wide landing (possibly originally another bedroom). A further, higher, landing gave access to two bedrooms and a dressing room. Here, the raising of the ceiling heights downstairs has caused the window sills to be only fourteen inches above floor level. Over the front door the porch is formed from a three- sided open arch decorated with trellis and the same profile is followed above in the dressing room, forming a bay window. There are signs of a former wrought iron open verandah in front of the parlour windows which is typical of the fashion of the period. It was later replaced by a glazed conservatory which was removed before 1920.

The Taylors sitting outside the house in about 1920

Enlargement

The second major extension and alteration took place about 1900 when an east wing was constructed in brickwork, rendered and colour washed to match the original, consisting of a music room on the ground floor leading off the parlour and a service passage and staircase leading off the kitchen which was relocated adjoining the servants' day room in the north east floor. The staircase enabled servants to reach their bedrooms at the rear of the house from corner of the house. A bedroom, dressing room and lavatory were also added to the first the kitchen without using the main staircase. There was also a door giving access to the music room from the service passage, now bricked up. Investigation of a number of layers of paint and paper has revealed remnants of the original stylised paintings of musical instruments, the original decoration of the music room. The new wing was reached on the first floor by an arch cut in the original wall leading to the service stairs and the new bedroom and dressing room. The most remarkable feature of this new work is its harmony with that of 1811, although it was carried out nearly a hundred years later. The addition of an oeil de boeuf window in the new bedroom, the inclusion of matching gothic windows and the projection of the new wing forward from the original adds to the feeling of asymmetry and authenticity of a Cottage Ornée.

The east wing
(See Colour Plate 35, Page 128)

Oeil de Boeuf window
(See Colour Plate 33, Page 127)

Decline

It seems that little of note in the way of alterations to the main structure took place in the period between the two world wars. After changing hands in 1912, the house was sold in 1920 and we know from the sale particulars that it was by then equipped with central heating, fired by a coal boiler located underneath the service passage built about 1900. This was quite early for a dwelling of this kind and some of the original cast iron radiators are still in use. The first bathroom was installed about 1900, when an additional WC in the east wing to supplement another in the west wing was built. The years of the 1939-1945 World War and its aftermath meant that both buildings and grounds suffered from neglect arising from lack of resources. In the 1950s there was little interest in period houses and many were demolished. A considerable amount of land was sold off during this period. When a sale of contents took place in 1955 part of the staircase collapsed from the weight of the number of potential bidders.

Restoration

The house was sold in 1955 to an agent who subsequently sold it on in 1956, whilst retaining much of the land and reducing the holding which had at one time exceeded twenty acres to two and three quarter acres. Much of the land sold consisted of cider orchards which flourished in the rich alluvial soil of the valley floor. When a derelict outbuilding was demolished some years ago the remnants of a stone cider press were discovered together with a number of stone mill wheels used for crushing the apple pulp. Although most of the land sold in 1955 was eventually used for the development of the bungalow estate in Blackmoor Close and Maysmead Lane, sufficient land remains to ensure privacy for a house of its size. Maysmead Cottage, originally used for housing servants, which is located in the north west corner of a formerly owned field at the west end of Greenwell Lane, was sold about 1979.

The new owners of 1956 carried out substantial repairs and alterations. On the ground floor the kitchen was moved to its present position on the west side of the house which had been previously used as a study. A large arch was constructed in the dividing wall between the parlour (now called the morning room) and the old kitchen which now formed a new study. The sitting room on the west side had by then become the dining room. A flat roof was built over part of the central courtyard at the rear for use as a store room, now a utility room. On the first floor, the wall between the main bedroom and the dressing room was removed and a new sash window inserted in the wall overlooking the side garden to the west of the house. An additional bathroom was installed in the large landing area to the right of the main stairs. A further bathroom was built in the dressing room of the east wing. Outside, the coach house was converted to a garage and outbuildings at the north east corner extended to form additional staff accommodation. Mains electricity was installed in 1928 and mains water in 1954.

Once more, the house was sold in 1964. The present owners purchased the house in 1976 and have carried out a number of alterations both before and since listing. In 1977 the very narrow stairs leading to the second floor were removed and replaced by a new flight leading from the principal bedroom to a dressing room and new en suite bathroom on the second floor. At the same time a conservatory was constructed on the west side of the house and the cloakroom was re-located in the former laundry room on the east side of the house. In 1983 an outside wash house was converted to a music studio. In 1990, the demolition of a derelict open-ended outbuilding and its rebuilding to the same profile, re-using original building materials, to cover an indoor swimming pool, the conversion of the adjoining coach house, used as a garage, to an exercise room and the construction at the rear of garages for three vehicles to replace asbestos cement structures was completed. In 1993, mains gas arrived in the village and a new boiler was installed and, in 2000, a glass-roofed atrium covering the major part of the courtyard at the rear of the centre of the house giving access to the music studio was erected. In 2005 work was completed on the removal of the service staircase in the east wing and the relocation of the en suite bathroom from the former dressing room to the area created on the first floor.

During the 1970s a trend developed in the village of sub-dividing the larger houses and building new dwellings in some of the larger gardens with surplus frontage. This was followed by applications to demolish some properties in order that the sites could be used to build several new houses. The local authority was concerned at the effect that these changes would have on the village-scape and in 1987, in common with many older dwellings in Lower Langford, which for some reason (probably administrative incompetence) were omitted from the original listings when the new Town and Country Planning Act originally came into effect, Maysmead Place was listed Grade 2. Subsequently, a Conservation Area was established which includes most of Lower Langford village and the whole of the land currently belonging to Maysmead Place.

The Garden and Grounds

With its setting in the middle of the Wrington Vale, and a view to Wrington in the north and to the south the towering heights of Blackdown, the highest point in the Mendips at over one thousand feet, the house must truly have looked in 1811 as if it was situated in a corner of Arcady. Indeed, the present view to the north must have changed little in the past two hundred years. Judging by the age of the mature trees in the grounds, a good deal of alteration and new planting was done at the turn of the 19th /20th Centuries when the east wing was added, resulting in a number of fine specimen trees surviving today.

On completion of the conversion of the House to a Cottage Ornée in 1811 the grounds were changed to a miniature of the sort of pleasure ground which a larger Regency house would probably have had. The dividing hedges to the fields in front of the

House were removed and a ha-ha (a hidden ditch with one vertical stone wall and one sloping bank, most of which still survives) constructed to divide the garden close to the House from the field which became parkland in which grazing cattle could be observed from the House without any visible fence or hedge. At the same time a winding gravel carriage drive, which is still in use, was constructed giving access from the lane.

When the present owners purchased the property some 30 years ago the garden was much overgrown and the house was barely visible under a mass of climbers. Over the years they have sought to retain as much of the original planting whilst introducing a greater element of formality appropriate to the Regency period in the form of some hard landscaping and the division into "rooms within a garden". New hard landscaping with formally shaped gravel paths and borders has been introduced but a serpentine woodland walk has been included in the overall plan. The enclosed vegetable garden has been converted into a Potager, or formalised mixed garden of flowers, vegetables, herbs and fruit, and a derelict greenhouse replaced by a restored period greenhouse. A new hedgerow using only native plants typical of the area has been planted at the northern boundary of the paddocks.

Owners past and present

Eliza Maria Armstrong - Owner (mid to late 19th century)
John Wilmot Bradford - Tenant
Alfred Bradford (Bombay Army) - Tenant
Harriet Hiscocks - Servant
Thomas Symes - Servant

William Charles Gallop (known as Charles)
and his wife Gertude L. Gallop (née Barnes) (late 19th century to 1912)
William Gallop and Charles Gallop (parents of William Charles)
Charity Dyer - Servant

Margaret Williams (1912 to 1920)

Mrs Taylor and Molly Taylor (1920 to 1955)

Colonel and Mrs Mardon (1956 to 1965)

Mr and Mrs Neville Copeman (1965 to 1976)

The Phillips (1976 to ?)

-22-

York Cottage

Jo Fryer

York Cottage is one of the oldest houses in Langford and possibly dates from the sixteenth century. It was one of the village shops for over ninety years.

York Cottage has been estimated to have been built between 1575 and 1640, and is believed to be one of the oldest properties in Langford. The cottage today shows three phases of its development. The front reception room, on the left as you enter the front door, is in the oldest part and has an inglenook fireplace with a bread oven. Within this room was the original staircase which no longer exists, but evidence of it can be seen along with the framework for its door. An old beam can be seen in the bedroom wall above, as well as large, old timbers in the loft space above. The walls in this part of the house are particularly thick and the doorways are probably 17th century.

The room to the right of the front door was used as a shop. It may have been extensively altered and extended, or even demolished and rebuilt since its original form. The property may have been a 'cross passage' cottage, with a room each side of a central passage way.

The rear of the property was probably added in Victorian times. The house originally had a thatched roof which was later changed to tiles.

The Deeds of the property give a lot of information. The house belonged to the Manor of Langford, the Reverend Thomas Whalley who leased it to John Emery, a baker, in 1791. The Rev. Whalley sold it in 1804 for £300 to Jeremiah Phillips, a dresser of leather. That same year John Bailey bought it and over the next six years the deeds indicate three more owners - John Morris 1810, James Thompson 1812 and John Whitely 1816. The deeds indicate that the property was sold to these four occupants but it is possible that they rented rather than owned, as in 1825, Edwin Phillips, the son and heir of Jeremiah Phillips, sold the house to James Weeks, a grocer, tea dealer and general shopkeeper.

By 1834 James Weeks was bankrupt and the property was sold to George Gane, a cheesemonger, for five shillings. When he died in 1846, York Cottage was mortgaged to Miss Mary Brookes. The census return for 1851 shows Daniel Underwood as occupier at York Cottage. As it was still in Mary Brookes' ownership, Daniel Underwood must have been renting it when it was sold to James Light in 1856. On the death of James in 1866, the mortgage was transferred to his son, Philip Light, who immediately sold it on to William Broackes.

York cottage appears as number 559 on the tithe map of 1842. The apportionment which accompanies it states that George Gane was the owner (confirming the information from the deeds) and Daniel Underwood occupied it . Daniel Underwood is recorded as 25 years of age and a grocer.

Part of the house had been converted to a grocery and drapery shop. The census returns of 1851 to 1901 give the following information:

Year	Name	Age	Occupation
1851	Daniel Underwood	37	Grocer
1861	Daniel Underwood	47	Shopkeeper
1871	Thomas Law	51	Draper and grocer
1881	Sarah Cox	40	Shopkeeper
1891	William Broackes	67	General shop man
1901	William Broackes	69	Draper and grocer

Census return 1851 - 1901

In 1841 Daniel Underwood, aged 25 years, was head of the household and lived with Anna, his wife and their children Edwin 2 and Henry 10 months. They had a female servant Mary Pipe.

In 1851 Daniel Underwood, at 37 years of age, was head of household and a grocer He lived at York Cottage with Ann his wife and their children William Henry 10, James 7, Emma 4 and Samuel 1. William Underwood aged 84 also appears on the census. This is likely to be Daniel's father. Harriet Manley, 22 years, is recorded as Daniel's niece and was a grocer's assistant. The household also had a servant Sarah Pipe aged 35 years.

In 1861 Daniel Underwood, at 47 years, is still recorded as head of the household and is described as a shopkeeper. He lived with Ann, his wife. Two of their children, Daniel E and Samuel, were living at home. Laura Ryall, a niece aged 23, was also living with them. Their servant Sarah Pipe still lived with them.

By 1871 York Cottage had changed hands and the head of the household was now Thomas Law who, at 51, is described as a draper and grocer. He lived with his wife Ann and they had a servant Harriet Lock aged 26 years.

In 1881 Sarah Cox, a forty year old widow, is recorded as shopkeeper. She was born in Bristol in 1840 and married Albert Cox, a draper and grocer. As the head of the household, she lived in York Cottage with her four children; Ada 13 years, William 12 years, Kate 11 years and Ernest 3 years.

In 1891 William Broackes appears in the census as head of household and general shop man. He had married Sarah Cox whose daughter, Kate Cox, aged 24 years, appears on the census as stepdaughter of William Broackes and is described as a shop assistant. William Broackes appears on the Deeds as having bought York Cottage in 1886 which makes it likely that he married Sarah, the tenant at York Cottage, that same year.

In 1901 William Broackes, aged 79 years, is still recorded as draper and grocer and lived at York Cottage with Sarah, his wife. They had a general servant Ellen Palmer who was 18 years old.

In 1905 William Broackes sold York Cottage to his stepson, Ernest Edwin Wood Cox, aged 27 years. He kept the shop as a general store with his sister, Ada Fanny, aged 37 years, who, by this time, was now Mrs Eley.

Shop prior to closing

Ernest Cox died intestate in 1934. The shop was passed to his sister, Ada Eley, who shut up the shop leaving all the stock inside. She sold it to a nephew, Kenneth William Mills. He sold it back to her in 1938 but she had no plans to reinstate the grocery business and the shop remained as it had been left when Ernest Cox died.

The shop remained untouched for 19 years until Mrs. Eley's death in 1953. The stock was just as it had been left in 1934. After her death, the property was sold to Albert Millior who had a huge task of cleaning up! The shop was cleared of all its stock and one of the Bristol newspapers ran a story about the 'Rip Van Winkle' shop.

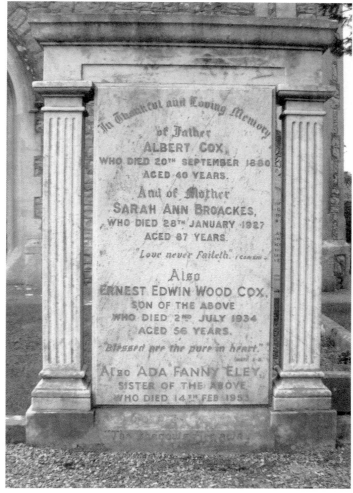

Grave of Sarah Cox, Ernest Cox, Ada Eley at Langford Chapel

In 1958 it was bought by a Dr and Mrs Knowlson who converted the shop part of the house back to a private residence. The shop windows were removed and the rooms that were once the shop were incorporated into the living space.

In 1979 York Cottage was sold to Mr. and Mrs. Anthony Robinson who sold it to Mr. and Mrs. Roy Cheater in 1997. In 2006 it was purchased by Bridget Woolstone and Dudley Lewis.

There is not much evidence that it was once a thriving village shop except it still has a large upstairs room which was once the storeroom. This covers the whole of the area above the shop. There is a bricked up opening on the side of the house, which was used for hauling in the stock.

What a different place Langford must have looked and what a leisurely pace of life there must have been when York Cottage was one of the many small shops in the area.

Exterior of store room

-23-

St Mary's House and Richmond House

John Gowar

As the history of these two Grade II-listed, Georgian houses is closely related, they are treated together in the following article. Sited on the north side of Langford Road, they have had many interesting owners and occupiers over the last 170 years. Those of whom there are reliable documentary records are featured here.

These two, fine, Grade II-listed, Georgian houses occupy a prominent position on the north side of Langford Road. Although they are detached from one another, they are separated by little more than a metre and their front facades are linked by a narrow curtain wall that rises almost to roof height. Richmond House has been known by that name for over 140 years: it is so named in a document of 1866 and in the 1881 Census and is shown as such on the 1885 Ordinance Survey map. In between times, it has also been called Richmond Villa. By contrast, St. Mary's House has had many names. In the same 1866 document, it is referred to as Maida Cottage. In the 1881 Census, it is called Mendip Villa, a name it retained until at least 1914. In more recent times, it has been Greystone. As that was almost identical to the name of another house in the village, it was changed in 1966 by the then occupants, Mr & Mrs Michael Phillips. The name St. Mary's related both to St Mary's Church and to Mrs Phillips' family home in Sussex[1]. In this article, we will use the name St. Mary's House throughout.

From external visual appearances, St. Mary's House seems to be the older of the pair. Its bold quoins and the design of the tops of the windows are typical of many houses built in Bristol in the 1760s. The windows themselves, 20-pane sashes on the ground floor and 16-pane sashes on the first floor, are typical of the late eighteenth and early nineteenth century and appear to retain the original glass. The remains of an early nineteenth century canopy can be seen along the west wall. On the large-scale Ordnance Survey maps, this is shown to have extended along the front of the house, where it would have been in keeping with the door now replaced by a French window. Also typical of the early nineteenth century are the wide bracketed eaves with diamond and circle patterning on the soffit board. Similar designs appear at Alden House and Langford Place.

The roof is very shallow, with two string courses. It is possible that the lower string course was the original roof level and that the roof was raised in the early nineteenth century. The lime-washed incised render of the front façade has been marked out to look like stone in a way that was fashionable from the 1770s to the 1820s. Although it is possible that the house was originally built in the mid-eighteenth century and was given a significant makeover in the 1820s, the North Somerset Register of Listed Buildings suggests that, in common with several other Langford houses, it was in fact newly built then. The ground plans shown in the tithe map of 1842 and the Ordnance Survey map of 1885 indicate a significant alteration to the back of the house between those dates.

In the Listed-Building Register, the pink-washed Richmond House is dated to about 1750 with early nineteenth century additions on the west side of the original building. These would have extended it towards St. Mary's House. The house has been subject to significant alteration over the years, the back of the house in particular having been

---

[1] Great care has to be taken with these house names. What is now Alden House is also shown on the 1st Edition large scale Ordnance Survey map (surveyed in 1883) as Mendip Villa, although in the revision of 1903 it is Mendip View.

enlarged between 1842 and 1885. Further changes, made between 1931 and the present day, can be seen from the thumbnail maps which also include Park Cottage and York Cottage. A covered passageway from the front door to the road is shown in the large-scale Ordnance Survey maps of 1885 and 1903 but is missing in the 1931 revision. Visually, the house does appear to be in two parts and the rendering is said to cover brick in one part and stone elsewhere. All the windows of the front façade are of similar design – twelve-pane sashes, though those of the end bay of the older part, the east end, are paired. The two pilasters on the west side of the façade are again typical of an early nineteenth century house.

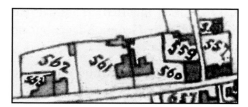

House map 1842

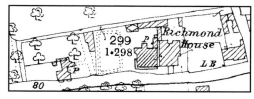

House map 1885

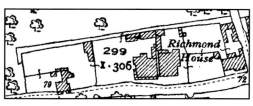

House map 1931

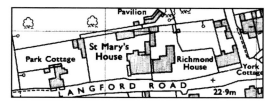

House map 1976

There is no known documentation to tell us who originally built these two houses, why they were built, or how they came to be built so close together. However, several deeds relating to the two properties form part of the archive of Langford House and have kindly been made available by Jean Darby. The earliest dates from 1806, but details from earlier documents of 1797, 1802 and 1803 are recited in some of the deeds. Together with the Tithe Apportionment Schedule of 1842, these documents give some information on how the ownership and occupation of the properties changed during the nineteenth century. Both houses are shown clearly on the Tithe Apportionment map for Churchill which, like its slightly earlier counterpart for Burrington, is the first plan of the village that enables individual properties to be specifically identified. The Tithe Schedule and the Census returns, made every ten years from 1841 to 1901, enable us to know who was occupying these houses on specific dates, although there are some uncertainties in basing the assignment of families to houses on the sequence in which the census returns were completed.

In the tithe apportionment schedule, Richmond House is plot number 560. The property is described as a house and garden occupying one rood and ten perches (really square perches), about 1500 sq. yds. The rent charge was two shillings and five pence per annum. The owner is given as Sir John Tylden and the occupier as Charlotte Synge, about whom more in a moment. Charlotte also occupied meadows, orchards and gardens of rather more than 10 acres on the other side of the turnpike road, extending to Langford Brook. These are the plots numbered 655, 656, 658 and 660 to 663 on the tithe map. They include a small cottage. Plot 663, the field known as Breach, was owned by the Rev. Samuel Simmons, the other land by Sir John.

St Mary's House is plot number 561. It, too, is described as a house and garden and occupied one rood and twelve perches, about 1570 sq. yds. It incurred an annual rent charge of two shillings and six pence. It was owned in 1842 by George Adams but no occupier is listed.

In the 1790s, both houses appear to have been part of the Langford Court estate, and so were part of the inheritance of Elizabeth Jones. In 1797, she and her second husband, the Rev. Thomas Sedgwick Whalley[2], sold one of these properties to James Simmons. He was a member of the distinguished army family which for many years occupied the house now called Somerlea. In 1803, they sold the freehold of an adjacent piece of land, which had previously been associated with the Green Dragon inn, to the Bristol-born solicitor, John Fisher (1776 – 1851). He came to own a great deal of land in Langford and was to build Langford House in the 1820s. Shortly afterwards, this second site was leased to James Simmons for 1000 years at a peppercorn rent. It is likely that it was part of the land whose income was used to fund the Edward Jones Charity in Burrington.

The documents indicate that John Fisher lived in one of the houses for a while, following a John Inman and being succeeded by James Simmons' sister Elizabeth Salmon. It is likely that John Fisher's son, John Thomas Fisher, who was to become Rector of Uphill and who would inherit Langford House, was born there in 1809. He died at

---

[2] The Rev. Whalley (1746 – 1828) receives a very bad press in many local publications. "Eccentric" and "profligate" are frequent epithets. Thomas De Quincey's acid comments on the luxurious appointments and lavish hospitality offered at Mendip Lodge are often quoted. (Perhaps he wasn't asked back.) The article in the Dictionary of National Biography offers a more balanced and sympathetic assessment and gives extensive first-hand references for those who would like to form their own opinion. He was, by all accounts, very tall, very thin, very learned, very generous and very hospitable. He travelled a great deal in Europe and kept journals of his experiences. He had three wives but no children. That he entertained lavishly, acquired expensive property and thereby spent a great deal of the considerable fortunes of the first two of his wives is not in dispute. But this attracted a distinguished artistic and intellectual circle to Langford. No doubt, when he came to sell off parts of the Langford Estate in order to fund this lifestyle, this was itself an attraction to the modestly wealthy professional and business men who were to build the houses we are describing here. It is recorded that he ended his life destitute, in poor lodgings, while wandering around France. In fact, I believe, he was visiting a favourite niece at La Flèche, just north of the Loire, when he died, aged 82, leaving a considerable fortune to charities, friends and relations.

IN MEMORY OF
AGNES JULIANA,
THE BELOVED WIFE OF Mʳ JOHN FISHER OF THIS PARISH.
WHO DEPARTED THIS LIFE ON THE 9ᵀᴴ DAY OF FEBRUARY 1832.
IN THE 53ᴿᴰ YEAR OF HER AGE.
HER REMAINS ARE DEPOSITED IN A VAULT.
IN THE SOUTH WEST CORNER OF THIS CHURCH

ALSO
IN MEMORY OF
THE BEFORE NAMED
JOHN FISHER,
FOR FIFTY YEARS A RESIDENT AT LANGFORD.
IN THIS PARISH.
HE DEPARTED THIS LIFE NOVEMBER THE SIXTH 1851,
AGED 76 YEARS.

HIS REMAINS ARE DEPOSITED
IN THE SAME VAULT.

ALSO LUCY ANN FISHER DAUGHTER OF THE ABOVE
DIED 22ᴺᴰ AUGUST 1900,
AGED 93 YEARS.

John Fisher's Memorial Tablet in St. John the Baptist's Church, Churchill

Langford House in July 1854, aged 44, leaving a wife and five children. John Fisher's wife, Agnes Juliana, had died in February 1832, presumably also at Langford House. In addition to John Thomas, they had a daughter, Lucy Ann, who remained unmarried and died in August 1900 aged about 94, having lived at various times in lodgings in Weston-super Mare, Bath and Clifton. Shortly before he died in November 1851, John Fisher, himself, appears to been involved in an accident on the railway, which resulted in him losing the use of his right arm.

In 1806, the freehold of this land was conveyed to a Peter Priest of Langford and the lease of one of the houses was sold to a gentleman from Bristol called Edward Stephens, to hold in trust for Peter Priest. Some of the remaining property is described as being "bounded to the north and west by a wall dividing it from a field called Lankland; to the south by the Bristol to Bridgwater Turnpike, and to the east by a garden owned by James Simmons and occupied by John Poole Tanner". Precise dimensions are given, but it is hard to reconcile them with any of the sites of which we have a record. It must be presumed that Lankland included the 18½ acre field numbered 567 on the tithe apportionment map and that it was renamed East Home Ground when John Fisher built Langford House. Both John Fisher and Peter Priest appear from the land-tax records to have had an interest in several "inns", so it is likely that the Green Dragon was one of these and was sited at or near to Richmond House or St. Mary's House. Peter Priest, who seems from his will to have been unmarried, died in 1825.

In June 1822, following the death of James Simmons, his heirs, his wife Sarah and his nephew Thomas Frederick Simmons, sold St. Mary's House to George Adams for £525. George Adams was also one of the trustees to whom the five acres of Middle Common was transferred under the provisions of the Simmons (or Symonds) charity. In 1828, the house was mortgaged and leased for a year, for £650, to a Bristol bookseller. This was Odiarne Coats Lane, who was to become Mayor of Bristol in 1861. In 1841, the house was occupied by a Mary Parker. Later, on 4th November 1845, George Adams, who had moved to Ross-on-Wye, was forced to sell it to Mr Lane for £400 in order to pay off part of his debt. In April 1846, it was sold again to one, George Price, who is described in census returns as a proprietor of property etc. He was born in London, married in Bristol and lived in Cardiff before moving to Weston-super-Mare. He continued to live with his family in Langford until he died in 1865 aged 67.

In the mean time, Richmond House had been acquired by Sir John Maxwell Tylden (1787 – 1866) of Milstead Manor, near Sittingbourne, Kent. He was a widower and had been a distinguished soldier, retiring from the army in 1825 with the rank of Lt-Col. He was a J.P. and became leader of the Liberal Party in east Kent. He was a strong supporter of catholic emancipation and parliamentary reform. He became deputy lieutenant of Kent in 1852.

Living in Richmond House in 1841 was Charlotte Synge (1789 – 1858) and her nephew Noah Hill Neale Synge (1811 - 1886). Charlotte became Sir John Tylden's second wife in 1842 and moved to Kent. Originally from Bridgnorth in Shropshire, the Synge family had strong Irish and ecclesiastical connections. Her father, Robert, was created a UK baronet on 12th August 1801 and died in 1804. Noah was the second son of her elder brother. He came to inherit the baronetcy in 1884.

By 1851, Richmond House was occupied by the curate of Burrington, the Rev. Thomas Jeffrey Bumpsted. Ten years earlier, he and his wife were living at Langford Lodge (now Milfort/Hylsbroke) where, in the tithe apportionment schedule he was described as both owner and occupier. It would appear that he sold this property and then rented Richmond House. Ten years later, he and his wife were living in the Rectory at Wrington together with their son James Jeffrey and his wife. James was also in holy orders but was without a living in 1861. In the census, he is described quaintly as "without cure of souls". The Rev. Thomas later became Rector of Dinder, where he died, aged 84, in 1883. At this time, the Perpetual Curate of Burrington and Rector of Wrington was the Rev. John Vane, who was then living in the Burrington Vicarage (now Burrington House). In his will, he appointed the Rev. James as one of his executors and he referred to his former curate as follows:-

I bequeath unto my friend The Reverend Thomas Jeffreys Bumpsted of Dinder near Wells (to whom money is no object) the sum of Sixty pounds in recollection of the cordial cooperation with me in the management of my Parish.

In June 1855, George Price bought what can only be Richmond House from Sir John and Lady Tylden for £350. He thus owned both houses. However, there is a mystery in the conveyance for this transaction in that the property is referred to as ....*all that messuage or tenement and dwellinghouse front court back yard walled garden and premises containing by admeasurement one rood and ten perches and numbered 557 on the Map and Survey of the said parish of Churchill which said messuage garden and premises are situate at Langford in the parish of Churchill in the County of Somerset and were lately in the occupation of the Reverend Thomas Jefferey Bumpsted....*

The Tithe Apportionment shows the site numbered 557 to be the now demolished cottage on the corner of the turnpike road and Redshard Lane (Maysmead) opposite York Cottage. In 1842, it was owned, like the rest of that area between Redshard Lane and Blackmoor, by Charles Granger and it measured 29 perches. It seems quite extraordinary that there should be such an obvious transcription error in such an important legal document but other explanations are hard to conceive.

In 1861, Richmond House was occupied by a widow, Maria Parker (73), who had previously farmed the 150-acre Bourne Farm between Burrington and Rickford. Maria died in 1867 at the age of 80. Note that this is not the Mary Parker who was living in St. Mary's House twenty years earlier. Staying with the Prices in St. Mary's House on census night, 7th April 1861, was Jane Plaister Baker, who had been brought up as a neighbour of Maria Parker in Bourne. Her father, Samuel Baker, was solicitor to the Smythe-Piggott estates. In 1862, George Price's younger son, Hans, married Jane. In 1866, Samuel Baker was stated to be living in Richmond House, though Mrs Parker is still listed in Kelly's Directory for that year.

When George Price died in March 1865, two of his sons were sheep farming, one in Natal and the other in Queensland. His widow, Eliza, his remaining son, Hans Fowler Price, and two of his daughters moved back to Weston-super-Mare. Hans lived first in Montpellier later

Hans Fowler Price (1835 – 1912)
(Courtesy of North Somerset Studies Library)

in Trewartha Park. He and Jane had five daughters and two sons. Jane died in 1889, Hans in 1912. Eliza and the daughters lived first in Royal Crescent, later on the Bristol Road, until Eliza died in 1896 aged 95. Hans was an architect and he designed many of Weston-super-Mare's late Victorian buildings, including the Old Town Hall, the old General Hospital, the School of Science and Art (which now houses the Hans Price Gallery of Weston College), Walliscote School and the Weston Mercury offices. He also designed the alterations to Somerlea.

In June 1866, the Price family auctioned both properties at Yatton. They were bought for £840 by a sugar refiner from London called Richard Dames, who had purchased Langford House two years earlier. He was unmarried at the time and would appear to have let both houses. He was born in Whitechapel in 1820 or 1821 and married a Mary Ann L. Matt at St. James's, Westminster, in the summer of 1868. Although he is listed in the 1872 Morris's Directory as still occupying Langford House, the 1871 census records him living with Mary Ann in London, in the Marylebone Road. Mary Ann died in Hungerford in 1909, aged 70, but Richard disappears from the records.

According to the 1871 census return, St. Mary's House was unoccupied. By 1881, both properties were again occupied by members of the same family. Elizabeth Tapscott, widow of a Clifton grocer, lived in St. Mary's House with her spinster daughter, Charlotte. Richmond House was occupied by her widowed daughter, Mary Jane Stone, with her two daughters and three sons. Elizabeth died in 1893, aged 83, and Mary Jane in 1904, aged 63. However, Charlotte was still living in St. Mary's House, and one of her nieces in Richmond House, in 1910. Charlotte died on 12th July 1912, aged 60. Her polished granite tombstone occupies a prominent position in front of the Churchill Methodist Church.

Charlotte Tapscott's tombstone at Churchill Methodist Church

There is a story that, at about this time, oatmeal was distributed from Richmond House to the poor of the neighbourhood through the generosity of Sidney Hill and possibly of Charlotte Tapscott too. While that cannot be confirmed, what is certain is that this house became the home and surgery of the local doctor for many years. This was Dr. Ernest George Douglas Pineo. He was born in Southsea in 1872 and had come to this area after qualifying. In 1901, he was living in Blagdon with his parents and older sister, Mabel. He was the first Chairman of Blagdon Village Club. It is likely that Dr. Pineo bought Richmond House when the last Miss Stone moved out following Miss Tapscott's death. He moved there from what is now Alden House and remained living there with his wife, Ella Elizabeth Mary, until his death in January 1942 at the age of 70. Among his many public services, Dr Pineo was Chairman of the Churchill and Burrington British Legion for many years.

IN MEMORY OF
ERNEST GEORGE DOUGLAS PINEO M.R.C.S. L.R.C.P.
CHAIRMAN OF THE CHURCHILL & BURRINGTON
BRANCH OF THE BRITISH LEGION 1923–1941
WHO DIED 7 JANUARY 1942
THIS TABLET WAS ERECTED BY HIS COMRADES
SERVICE NOT SELF

The memorial tablet to Dr Pineo in St John the Baptist's Church, Churchill

Dr Ernest Pineo
(Courtesy of Blagdon History Society)

One of Dr and Mrs Pineo's daughters, Mrs Rosemary Corpe, was in the Philippines at the outbreak of World War II and was taken prisoner by the Japanese. She had a daughter, Rose and a son Crispin, who was disabled, it is said, as a result of the harsh treatment received by Rosemary while in captivity. On their return, they lived in Mill House, Rickford. The Pineos' other daughter, Felicity, married a Victor Cross. According to a document of May 1946, Ella Elizabeth Pineo was then still living in Richmond House and lent her son-in-law the sum of six hundred and eighty-seven pounds, eleven shillings and eight pence towards the purchase of Laburnum House (now Nash House).

Shortly after this, Richmond House was occupied by David and Elizabeth Williams and their family. David was an officer in the RNVR and he and his brother are believed to have run an engineering business in the north of Bristol. In May 1958, he became the 4th Baronet Williams of Bridehead in Dorset and the family returned to his family home. Audrey Morris, who lives at Churchill Gate remembers visiting her cousin at Richmond House, where she was nanny to the Williams children. Sir David Williams died in 1970, aged 61. Elizabeth's family estate was Tyneham, which was requisitioned by the War Office and never returned. She was to become High Sheriff of Dorset in 1979 and was recently still living in the county, at Owermoigne.

Subsequently, Richmond House has passed through the hands of several owners and seen much internal alteration. Those who have lived there since the mid-1950s include several families who are well known to or will be remembered by many residents of Langford:

> Mollie Mansell, who was the sister of Mrs Norman Tricks;
>
> Tony and Anne Robinson (1962 to 1981 - Anne still lives nearby in Wrington);
>
> Sally Logie (1981 to 1997), who still lives opposite in Roemarten.
>
> The previous owners were Nathan and Catrin Butcher.

There is less certainty about the earlier 20th-century owners and occupiers of St. Mary's House. A Mrs Broad was in residence in the 1930s; her butler was a Mr Doughty. Dora Tanner, an American lady with two children, lived there in the 1950s; her housekeeper/cook was Minnie May Jeffery. Sally and John Baker lived there in the early 1960s. One of John's sisters is Lady Jane Wills; another married Richard Hill, whose family owned the Bristol shipyard and who lived at The Forge. Mr and Mrs Michael Phillips came to St. Mary's House in 1966 and sold it to Mollie and Peter Kemp in 1976, when they moved to Maysmead Place. The present occupant, Patrick Lawson, moved from the Rectory in Wrington in 1979.

Date	Richmond House	St. Mary's House
June 6th, 1841	Charlotte Synge (50) and Noah Neale Synge (25) with one male and three female servants.	Mary Parker (55) with one male and one female servant. (Not Maria Parker)
March 30th, 1851	Thomas Jeffery Bumpsted (52), curate of Burrington, with wife, Frances (54), three male students and three female servants.	George Price (53), with Henry Meredith, son (24), Selina, daughter (23), Louisa, daughter (14), Eliza Ann, daughter (11) and two female servants.
April 7th 1861	Maria Parker (73) with 1 female servant.	George Price (63),with wife Eliza (59), son Henry Meredith (34), daughter Selina (33), son Hans Fowler (25), a visitor, Hans' future wife, and two female servants.
April 2nd, 1871	Mary Dennison (44) with son William A. U. (16) and two female servants.	Uninhabited, to be let.
April 3rd, 1881	Mary J. Stone (widow, 41), with daughters Elsie (11) and Lucy L. (10), sons George H. (7), Charles G. (5) and Alfred A.S.D. (3), and one female servant.	Occupant away. (Elizabeth & Charlotte Tapscott were visiting in Bristol).
April 5th, 1891	Mary J. Stone (widow, 51), with daughters Margaret E. (25), Winifred M. (22) and Elsie (21), son George H. (19), and one female servant.	Elizabeth Tapscott (widow, 80), with daughter Charlotte (39) and one female servant.
March 31st, 1901	Mary J. Stone (widow, 61), with daughters Margaret E. (35) and Elsie (31), son George H. (27), and one female servant.	Charlotte E. Tapscott (49) and one female servant.

Occupiers from Census Returns

-24-

Somerlea House

Clare Smith

Somerlea is of Georgian origin with the original part of the house being built in approximately 1785. The house was then greatly extended in 1874 which is in true Victorian style and is the east aspect of today's house.
In the years 1906-1913 the Georgian part of the house underwent major alterations which included the removal of the front door from the north to the east side and the building of the grand staircase in the original library hence linking the Georgian and Victorian wings.

Somerlea began life as its own small country estate. Tithe maps of the time showed the house with lawn and gardens totalling two acres, with two stables and a carriage house alongside. Adjacent to the house were seven acres of pasture, seven acres of meadow and seven acres of fern. It is believed that the estate was built by the Simmons family as their main residence as they are linked to other properties in the area. Members of the family occupied Somerlea throughout the 19th century.

The 1841 census for Churchill parish shows Frances Simmons (75) as the landowner being of "independent means". Other family members named include Thomas, son, an army lieutenant, Mary his wife, their son Egbert and three house servants.

A Georgian window in the house still retains the etching into glass of "Surgeon to the forces" Easter 1845, showing an obvious house guest and colleague of Thomas Simmons.

The 1861 census for the parish shows Mary Simmons now aged 68 and her son Charles aged 43, a solicitor, residing at Somerlea along with three servants and a gardener. One of the servants was named Elizabeth Lintern and it is strange to note that by the 1881 census Mary Simmons had deceased and, the house now belonged to Charles Lintorn Simmons age 63, a solicitor and J.P. for Somerset! In 1874 Sir Lintern Simmons extended Somerlea with a Victorian wing (see attached plan).

The 1861 census for the parish shows Mary Simmons now aged 68 and her son Charles aged 43, a solicitor, residing at Somerlea along with three servants and a gardener. One of servants was named Elizabeth Lintern, which is strange, as Lintorn is a family name of the Simmons. By the 1881 census, Mary Simmons had died but the house was still occupied by Charles Simmons, age 63, a solicitor and J.P. for Somerset. In 1874, Sir (John) Lintorn Simmons extended Somerlea with a Victorian wing designed by Hans Price (see plan on page 206).

The house remained in the Simmons family until 1902 when it became the home of the two 'Miss Christie' sisters, who were related to Sidney Hill of Langford House. The Miss Christies then undertook nine years of major alterations to the house which included raising the floor levels, re-opening existing windows and the addition of carved wooden fire places in several of the principal rooms. Much of the work and details were carried out in the Arts and Crafts style which replaced the Victoriana.

In the late 1940s, Somerlea was bought by the King family. Tom King their son was a local M.P. for Bridgwater and is now the Rt. Hon. Lord King having served for many years as a cabinet minister in Margaret Thatcher's Government. It was enjoyed very much as a family home with croquet and the church fete held on the main lawn. Mrs King sold Somerlea in 1975 to Tony Fowles and family (see Chapter 3). Tony was a wartime evacuee who pioneered a new type of scaffolding. He then sold it to Clare and David Smith the present owners in 1997. It remains a family home today.

On the south aspect of the house the Georgian windows were altered to create large bay windows and extend the room size hence the only remaining Georgian feature is the north side.

Georgian windows altered to bay windows

The scullery had installed two large hand pumps which were used daily by the servants to fill a large tank on the first floor for the household to use.

Two servants hand pumps

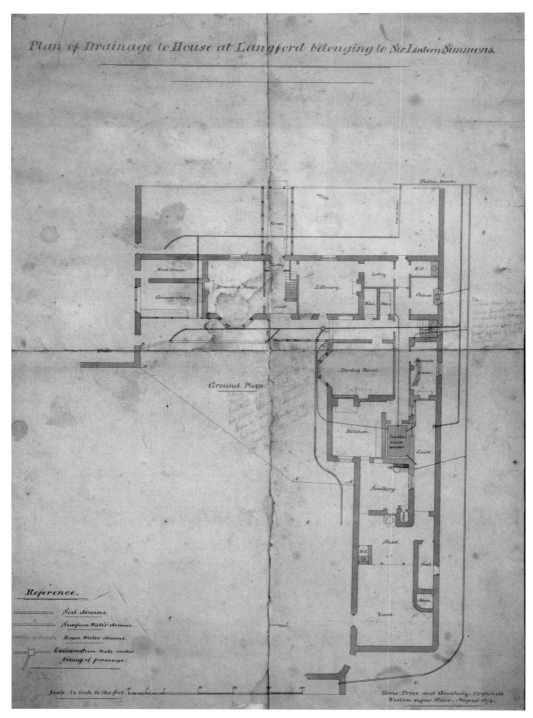

Map of Somerlea including drainage plans 1874
(See Colour Plate 36, Page 129)

-25-

Langford House

Jo Fryer and Jean Darby

Until the mid 1940s Langford House was a private residence. The property is most often associated with Sidney Hill who was Langford's generous benefactor. Today people think of Langford House as the Veterinary College which is part of The University of Bristol. Fortunately the building remains in good condition and many of its original features can still be seen today.

Langford House is a large former country house built in the Italianate style. It has two storeys. The east front has three bays with the central one projecting forwards.

There have been additions to the south west and north east including a belvedere tower.

The house has tall window openings with shouldered and eared architraves and keystones. The windows are made of plate glass and are sash.

Langford House was first built and owned by John Fisher (born 1781) who bought land known as 'Hills' from Thomas Sedgwick Whalley in 1826. He used 3 acres 1 rood and 39 perches of the 10 acres purchased to build his house, outbuildings, garden and lawn. At this time the house had no front drive.

John Fisher died in 1851 and his son the Reverend John Thomas Fisher, who was born at Langford in 1804, inherited Langford House. He lived there for six years before his death in 1857.

In 1857 the trustees of the Reverend John Thomas Fisher sold the freehold estate called Langford House and 'parcels of land' comprising in total 54 acres 1 rood and 32 perches. The purchaser was the Reverend Henry Richards.

From the census in 1861 we know it was lived in by Edward Griffiths Richards and his family. Edward Richards was a late captain in the militia and also a J.P.

In 1864 the property was sold to Richard Danes. In 1866 he also purchased Richmond House and Mendip Villa (now St. Mary's House).

The 1871 census shows Captain Vihacey Wooldridge, age 31 (a captain unattached in the Light Infantry) occupying Langford House. He would appear to be renting the property. He is recorded as living with his wife Jane, age 27, who had been born in the Cape of Good Hope where their first son James was born. Their next three sons, Leizer 5, William 3 and Herbert 1 were born in the West Indies.

By 1874, three messuages and land on Langford House Estate were sold to William Turner.

Clock tower
(See Colour Plate 37, Page 130)

In 1877 the entire Estate was purchased by Simon Sidney Hill. He spent money on enlarging and embellishing Langford House converting it into an imposing mansion and park. He rebuilt the house in an Italian style, added the tower, outhouses, stables and a dairy. He installed a gilt clock above the coach House and this could be heard playing 'All Things Bright and Beautiful' to mark every hour as well as chiming the half and quarter hours.

The interior was decorated in the typical flamboyant Victorian style with dark paint and panelling.

Victorian interior

Sidney Hill specialised in breeding Red Scotch Shorthorn cattle and the sheds he built for them in the 1890s were nicknamed the 'Bullock Palaces' as each animal had its own house with a dormer window and 'mod cons' in advance of their time.

The 'Bullock Palaces'

He died in 1908 after living at Langford House for over 30 years. His nephew Thomas James Hill was left the property in the Will, for his life, but he died after four years. James A Hill inherited it but decided not to take up residence. It was passed to Thomas Sidney Hill who was the son of Thomas James Hill and great nephew to Simon Sidney Hill.

When Thomas Sidney Hill died in 1944, his son Ronald inherited Langford House but did not wish to take on the burden of running the estate, so the house and grounds were put on the market.

In 1946 the Commissioners of Crown Land purchased the Estate. In 1948 the University of Bristol set up its School of Veterinary Science and its first student vets started in Bristol in 1949.

By 1951 Bristol University had bought the Langford House Estate and established the School of Veterinary Science with a Clinical school and a Teaching Hospital plus Laboratories. The first students arrived in 1953.

There were other developments parallel to this. The Somerset Breeding Centre was set up in 1948. They leased land and an Artificial Insemination Unit was set up.

In 1949 part of the Ministry of Agriculture, Fisheries and Food moved from Bristol to Langford and they financed a Meat Research Institute from 1968 until 1990. The Institute was opened by the Queen, and local people gave her a great welcome. A decorative arch was erected across the road at the corner of Stock Lane and was inscribed 'God Bless the Queen'. The trees had red and white bunting linking them, and people decorated their houses along the royal route.

Today the University's Veterinary School is used to train final year and post graduate students. It is internationally renowned for its vast expertise.

Although Langford House is no longer a private residence it has kept many of its original features. The outside of the house has not changed. The inside is used for offices, teaching and conferences. Many of the rooms have the original ornate wooden panelling and ceilings as well as cornices and architraves.

The main difference today is in the amount of land owned by the Estate. In 1826 when John Fisher built his house it was just over three acres. Today the Langford House Estate owns about 220 acres.

The Two Sidney Hills of Langford House

An article about Langford House would not be complete without further detail about Simon Sidney Hill and his great nephew Thomas Sidney Hill. Both were exceptional men who were kind hearted and demonstrated great public spirit. They were both loved by the people they lived amongst and were considered to be benefactors to Langford and Churchill.

Simon Sidney Hill on a horse

The first Sidney Hill

Simon Sidney Hill was born in Clifton, Bristol in 1829. He became a draper in Bristol until he had to give it up before he was 30, through ill health. His doctor advised him to take a sea voyage and he set sail for New Zealand. When he reached Cape Town he decided to stay and he entered into partnership with Mr William Savage in Port Elizabeth. Their business was called Savage Hill and they were colonial and general merchants who pioneered the South African trade. They traded in minerals and other things, one of which was ostrich feathers for the fashion trade and haberdashery industry.

The business prospered and Sidney Hill was beginning to make his fortune. After 7 years he returned to England in abundant health and great wealth. He directed his firm's large shipping interests from London.

Simon Sidney Hill

Mary Ann Bobbett

On 15th June 1864, aged 35, Sidney Hill married Miss Mary Ann Bobbett (born 1838) whom he had met while she was keeping house for her uncle, Mr William Bobbett, in Bristol. The Bobbett family were from Bristol and were flour distributors and bakers. Sidney Hill arranged for a licence for weddings to be granted for the old Methodist chapel and he and Mary Ann Bobbett were the first to marry there.

The following year they sailed for Port Elizabeth to set up home in South Africa. Sidney Hill decided to lavish some of his money on a chapel for Wesleyan Methodists in South Africa. The building in Port Elizabeth was finished in 1872.

Mary Bobbett's health failed and they returned to England in 1874. Unfortunately Mary died within a few months, in Bournemouth, and was buried at Arnos Vale Cemetery in Bristol.

Sidney Hill was grief stricken over his wife's death. He returned to South Africa but could not settle. He came home again in 1877 and bought Langford House.

Sidney Hill funded the building of a new Wesleyan Methodist Church in Churchill in memory of his wife. The old chapel was pulled down to make way for the new one and services were held in the School Room. In 1881 Mary Ann Bobbett's remains were removed from Arnos Vale and placed in a mausoleum in front of the Church. Each Sunday, before the service, Sidney Hill would place a rose on his wife's grave.

Mausoleum of Mary Ann Bobbett

Sidney Hill severed all connections with his world of trading. He settled into a new life as a gentleman farmer taking great care of his animals. He had advanced ideas for his day about agriculture.

Sidney Hill was extremely generous with his money. He was always ready to help the poor and sick and to provide for widows and orphans. Sidney Hill would notice the poor and make enquiries about them. A note would be given to them to take to the Post Office in Churchill. The two upstairs rooms were full of household items provided by Langford House. Mr Carter, the proprietor, would follow the instructions in the note and supply blankets, boots or whatever was required.

Children who attended the Methodist Sunday School were given a set of clothes each Christmas. The poor families were dependent on this.

He treated his staff extremely well. For a month each year the people of Langford House and their servants went on holiday. The servants were able to relax just as much as the family. He became known as 'Mr Great Heart' for all his good deeds and generosity.

As well as helping people he paid for the following:

Wesleyan Methodist Church, Churchill plus fund for upkeep

Memorial Sunday Schools (adjoining the chapel)

Victoria Jubilee Homes, Langford plus £30pa for residents and fund for upkeep

Methodist Chapels at Shipham, Sandford, Blagdon and Cheddar

Churchill Clock Tower

Churchill Cottage Homes plus funds to support residents and for upkeep

He also provided and furnished manses at Banwell and Cheddar as well as contributing to the funds of Churchill Parish Church.

There was only ever one hint of dissension concerning Sidney Hill's good deeds. This was when he had the small cottages close to the Nelson Inn pulled down. He felt they were too near the Inn and would provide too great a temptation for those living there and that they would drink away their earnings. He built the Cottage Homes in Front Street and paid the new occupants a weekly sum to live there. An oak tree, with railings around, was planted where the cottages had been.

Sidney Hill lived the last 30 years of his life at Langford House. He had always enjoyed good health but, returning from church on 26th January 1908, he fell in his hall and fractured his thigh. It seemed to be healing well but he caught influenza which turned to pneumonia. After five weeks he died peacefully on 3rd March 1908, aged 79 years.

His funeral service was to have been held in the Methodist Church, but, despite the blustery wind, it was decided to hold it in the open as huge crowds were anticipated. Family and friends would be present as well as professional and business associates from Bristol and further away. It was anticipated that almost the entire population of the Wrington and Cheddar valleys would be attending.

The blinds and curtains were drawn in all the houses and cottages in Langford and Churchill. The coffin was borne by the carriage which he always used to go to church in and was drawn by his favourite bay horse. It was preceded by eight carriages containing his immediate family followed by a long procession of six more horse drawn carriages containing more family (nephews, nieces, great nephews and great nieces), his brothers-in-law and his sister-in-law, some of his staff (his steward, private secretary) and vicars from across the local area. Behind them was a huge funeral procession on foot. This was headed by the Estate's outdoor staff, the local Wesleyans, representatives of village organisations, Sunday school children and the Banwell Fire Brigade.

There were so many beautiful wreaths with heartfelt messages.

'In affectionate and loving memory of the best and kindest of masters
From the indoor and outdoor staff on the Langford House Estate'

'In affectionate remembrance of a loving and devoted super-intendant
for over 31 years
from the assistant super-intendant, teachers and scholars of
the Churchill Wesleyan Memorial Sunday School'

Simon Sidney Hill was buried in the same grave as his wife at the Wesleyan Methodist

The funeral of Simon Sidney Hill 1908

church. Flags flew at half mast and after the burial the bell ringers muffled their peals.

Sidney Hill had been a very religious man, several Wesleyan ministers shared the funeral service. The Rev. W. Perkins of London, who had known Sidney Hill for over 20 years and had often stayed at Langford House, paid a moving tribute at the graveside.

The great blow which you have long dreaded and which some of you have for a long time seen descending, has fallen at last and you are here this afternoon, the living of many generations, from many homes, young and old, gathered round your dead in a last simple solemn service. With some of you it is the latest service of many you have shared with him.

Many of you will be seeing him as you used to see him in the adjoining house of prayer, the man you knew and loved, worshipping reverently, either in his own pew or seated with the boys, joining earnestly in prayer, and listening in rapt attention, with eyes sometimes filled with tears, to the message of the gospel.

I think I hear from that coffin breaking the stillness of death, the voice of our dear friend saying 'Friends of mine, from many places, friends of mine among whom I have loved for years, when you come together round my coffin, sing hymns of praise to God. Say very little about me, but say much about Him. Speak of the mercy that inspired and strengthened me in every good thing I did, that comforted me in age and weakness.'

Looking back on his life, it was a very happy one, long though it was, and clouded with a great sorrow written on the marble close by. Yet Mr Hill was something of a paradox, for the great sorrow of his life was also a great happiness. Just think, his joy in having one sweet, sacred memory, to have one loved face, never hidden through all the mists of years, was enough to make a man's heart burst with joy, even while tears were flowing down his cheeks. He never, never forgot his young wife.

The poor found in Mr Hill a friend to whom they never appealed in vain. His memory will live among you for generations, and your children's children will come and read the name on the stone and listen to the story of a good man's life, a man who had friends, who loved him all over the world, but his supreme sympathy was with the poor people of his own Mendip countryside, the children, the fatherless, the helpless, the weak, the sick. They have lost the best and truest friend they have ever had. I pray that God will raise up others to carry on the great work our friend has done.

Sidney Hill was generous in life and now his Will showed him to be generous in death. He left legacies to his long serving staff, many of whom he named in his Will, having decided how much his gift would be. Other servants were left money ranging from £8 to £30 depending on their length of service. He also left substantial amounts to his family.

The Estate was left in his will, to his nephew Thomas James Hill for the duration of his life. Thomas James Hill lived at Langford House for just 4 years before he died in

1912. The terms of the will were that the next beneficiary was James A Hill, another of Sidney Hill's nephews. He never took up residence and so Langford House was passed to Thomas Sidney Hill, the son of Thomas James Hill. He was Simon Sidney Hill's great nephew.

The second Sidney Hill

Thomas Sidney Hill had been born in Durban, South Africa in 1874, was brought to England at an early age and grew up in Bristol.

Thomas Sidney Hill had married Edith Emily Albury. After his father's death, they moved into Langford House with their two children, Thurle and Ronald, in 1913. In 1914 his younger daughter Daphne was born, completing his family.

Like his great uncle Simon Sidney Hill, he lived the life of a gentleman farmer and he

Thomas Sidney Hill and Edith Emily Albury

too, spent time and money furthering public welfare and was a generous benefactor to the local area. He was prominent in district and county public life.

He had learnt engineering while he was living in Bristol and was a very practical man. He realised that motor cars would revolutionise life and he joined a well known firm of motoring engineers. To publicise a particular car he successfully drove it up one of the steepest gradients in Bristol (Ninetree Hill). In the early days of motoring, car engines were notoriously unpredictable and his success caused quite a sensation. Sidney Hill owned the first car in this area. He opened the Langford by-pass in 1932 and was the first to drive along the new road. Sidney Hill was also the first to have a telephone and to own a tractor.

Sidney Hill's farming interests centred around his pigs. He bred pedigree Berkshires which were housed in his great uncle's 'Bullock Palaces'. He encouraged his farming neighbours by giving innumerable lavish prizes for agricultural and flower shows, many of which were held on the Estate grounds at Langford House.

In 1913 Sidney Hill enlarged Langford House by adding a new wing to provide a billiard room and nursery. He loved playing billiards and one of his most prized possessions was a cue given to him by John Roberts, the greatest player of his day. He also added the Belvedere Tower and a dairy. The back entrance (tradesman's entrance) to Langford House was from Maysmead. It has been in Stock Lane only since the university have owned it.

Sidney Hill was a talented sportsman. When he was young he had been a full-back for Bristol Rugby Club. The sport that he was passionate about was cricket. He was a good all rounder and could have played for Somerset but his many self-imposed public duties came first.

He created one of the finest private cricket grounds in the country at Langford House. It had the latest type of scoring board and a wonderful pavilion. When he no longer played cricket Sidney Hill would watch the matches from the viewing gallery of the Belvedere tower he had built. The Langford players showed their appreciation when they presented him with a silver salver with the names of the club members on it. The cricket pitch served as an inspiration to other clubs who gradually got rid of their bumpy pitches and jungle like outfields.

Langford House cricket team plus the Hill Family, 1922

Sidney Hill's generosity included giving weekly gifts of food, blankets, clothes and shoes to the poor. Records were kept of Christmas gifts so that villagers would not receive the same gift two years running.

During the First World War there were huge gatherings of wounded soldiers in the summer months when Langford House was used as a makeshift hospital. At Christmas there were groups of Australian soldiers at Langford House. They were very appreciative of the roast beef (from a prize winner), abundant vegetables and Christmas pudding served on Christmas Day.

Sidney Hill had a pioneer interest in wireless telegraphy and became secretary of the Advisory Board the BBC set up in Bristol. He was extremely pleased when his son Ronnie Hill became a broadcaster.

One of Sidney Hill's interests was photography, especially using a ciné camera. At one time he was the only person in Langford to own a camera. During the 1920s to 1940s he made several amateur films of scenes of his family at Langford House, local people, places and events.

Fetes were a regular feature at Langford House. The fete in 1937, to celebrate the Coronation of George VIth, was captured by Sidney Hill on film. There are scenes of the procession of local people up the drive, the band playing, the fancy dress competition (in which his daughters Thurle and Daphne were dressed as policemen) and the country dancing display. During the morning of the Coronation, Sidney Hill presented all the children up to fourteen years of age with souvenir mugs. These and the children's and adults' teas were all funded by Sidney Hill.

Sidney Hill employed many staff at Langford House. There were farm workers, carpenters, gardeners, nurses, a governess and maids. A house as large as Langford House would have up to five maids – the head housemaid, the under housemaid, the parlour maid, the under parlour maid and a general maid. The staff were well looked after and each year a staff outing would be arranged with everyone travelling by charabanc. The Hills would have a month's holiday each year and their servants would accompany them.

Langford House estate workers' outing, 1922

The children, Thurle, Ronnie and Daphne would have lessons in the morning with their governess, Miss Young, where they learned spelling, maths, history and geography. The eldest daughter, Thurle, proved to be artistic and a special teacher was employed to teach drawing. The lessons were held in the morning room. At the end of the morning the children would have lunch with their parents followed by an afternoon walk. They had their tea with their two nurses in the nursery.

The Hills entertained frequently at Langford House, holding large tea and dinner parties. The 'best' local people were invited as well as people from Bristol. At eighteen, the children were allowed to have dinner with their parents and guests, and were expected to help entertain the visitors.

Sidney Hill was a tubby, jolly man and Mrs Edith Hill was very tall (thought to be six feet four inches) and always bent her legs in company in order to speak on the same level.

Sidney Hill suffered from heart problems and when he became very ill he was confined to bed for the last 3 years of his life. He died in 1944 aged 70 years.

Langford House was left to Ronald Hill, his son but he did not want to live in it and the era of Langford's benefactors came to an end.

Glossary

Taxes and tithes

Hearth tax

This tax was implemented in 1662 and was charged at two shillings a hearth paid twice yearly. The tax inspectors had to enter the property to count the number of hearths. Any attempt to avoid tax by blocking up a chimney would result in the tax being doubled if they were discovered. It was abolished in 1696.

Window tax

This was an unpopular tax introduced in 1696 and replaced the hearth tax. The windows in a property were counted from the outside and any more than six were liable for tax. A flat rate of two shillings was charged for seven to nine windows and four shillings for ten to nineteen in 1792 for example. Many people felt this was a tax on fresh air, light and health and to dodge paying the full amount people would brick up some of their windows. In 1825 the number of windows taxable was increased to over eight. In 1851 the window tax was abolished.

Land tax

This was a tax on personal estates, public offices and land that people owned and was first imposed in 1692. Between 1780 and 1832 returns were sent to the Clerk of Peace for the Quarter sessions, when they were used to indicate those entitled to vote in the Parliamentary elections. A record was kept of all tax payers in the form of annual lists. The information listed the houses (but not always their names), the owners and occupiers, a brief description of the property as well as the tax paid. The tax was finally abolished in 1969.

Tithes

Tithes date back to the tenth century or earlier when everyone had to pay ten percent of their annual produce from the land or labour. This was to support the parish priest, maintain the parish church and support the poor of the parish. Detailed tithe maps were produced in the mid nineteenth century. Each property was given a number and plotted on the tithe map. The accompanying apportionment (list) gave the name of the owner and tenant if applicable, size of property and amount of tax payable.

Census

A census is a population survey taken every ten years from 1801. It is only since 1841 that the names of occupiers were recorded. They name everyone living in the house on the night the survey took place and give ages, place of birth (from 1851) and occupations. They are only released when one hundred years have passed.

Terms associated with property, land and deeds

Annuitant
A person in receipt of an annuity.

a. r. p. (acres, roods and perches)
This stands for acres, roods and perches which measure area land. They are always quoted on the tithe apportionment and feature on house deeds.

A square perch (usually just referred to as 'perch') is the smallest area of land measured.

It is interchangeable with the terms rod and pole. In the 12th century the word 'perch' was derived from the Latin 'petrica' meaning a measuring rod or pole and was measured from the back of a plough to the front of the oxen. Until the measurement was standardised the length of a linear rod, in the 15th century, was the combined length of the feet of 16 men as they left church on a Sunday morning!

A rood was traditionally the area of a narrow strip of land equivalent to 0.25 acre.

An acre was originally a measurement of area from the 13th century and was traditionally the area of a strip of land (40 rods x 1 rod) that a yoke of oxen could plough in one day.

Perches, Roods and Acres	Imperial Equivalents
40 square perches = 1 rood	1 square perch = 30.25 square yards
4 roods = 1 acre	1 rood = 1210 square yards
	1 acre = 4840 square yards

Abstract of title
This is a summary of prior title prepared when a property was sold.

Chattels
This is personal property.

Codicil
This is a signed and witnessed addition to a will.

Conveyance
A conveyance is a deed which transfers property (as well as land) from one owner to another.

Covenant

This is an agreement creating an obligation entered into by one of the parties and features on the deeds.

Dower

A widow's share for life of her husband's estate.

Executor/executrix

This is a male or female person appointed to carry out the provisions of a will.

Indenture

An indenture is a document written in duplicate on the same parchment or paper which was then divided in two by cutting a wavy line.

Inclosure/enclosure

Common land, open fields and land belonging to the Church (glebe land) were divided up into allotments and distributed amongst relevant claimants in order to make agriculture more efficient. It frees the land from common rights.

Leasehold

A leasehold is for a fixed number of years or a certain number of 'lives' recorded in the original lease. When one of the 'lives' died, a new name could be substituted into the lease for payment of a fee.

Messuage

In property law this was any dwelling house with outbuildings and land assigned to its use.

Quarter days

25th March = Lady Day	4th June = Midsummer
29th September = Michaelmas	25th December = Christmas

Tenement

In property law this was any kind of permanent property such as land, dwellings etc.

Tenure

This is the condition or form of right by which a property is held or occupied.

Architectural terms

Bressemer
This is a timber beam.

Cottage Ornée
This was an artfully small house associated with the picturesque movement.

Cornice
A cornice is a continuous horizontal projecting courde or moulding at the top of a wall or ceiling.

Cyma
This is a moulding with a double curve part concave part convex.

Dentil
A dentil is one of a number of small square or rectangular blocks forming an ornamental detail often under a classical cornice on a building.

Ha-ha
This was a retaining wall sunk into a ditch in a landscape garden or park and used to make a barrier without disrupting the view.

Gothick
'Gothick' was a revival of the Gothic style of the 12th century. It was in evidence from the 17th to 19th Centuries and at its peak from 1730-1780. Its revival came at a time when there was a desire for novelty and change and a hankering for the romantic and picturesque. It used thin, delicate forms with little concern for archaeological accuracy or structural logic. It featured medieval details, gable ends with barge boards to protect the roof from wind and rain and windows with pointed Gothic arches.

Palladian
Much of the 17th century architecture was influenced by the work of Andrea Palladio (1508 – 1580). He revived and developed a classical style and was greatly influenced by ancient Rome. His architecture was symmetrical and harmonic in its proportions.

Architectural Periods

Medieval
Medieval dates from the late 11th century to the late 15th century.

Tudor

The Tudor period was from 1485-1603. It is noted for its simplified perpendiculars, steep gables, tall chimneys and straight headed mullion windows.

Elizabethan

Elizabethan relates to the late 16ᵗʰ century. It was a time when there was decorative use of Renaissance ornament, and lots of symmetrical facades and gables similar to and often undistinguishable from Jacobean. Many large and tradional country houses were built in an 'E' shape.

Jacobean

This was called after James 1st from 1603-1625 and was still common in the middle decades of the 17ᵗʰ century. It used densely applied classical ornament and symmetrical gabled facades.

Georgian

This period covers Kings George I, II, III, IV from 1714 – 1830. It is known for its classical style and proportions. Its architecture was distinctive with its shallow pitched roofs and the introduction of sash windows.

Regency

This was a late Georgian period of architecture from 1800-1830. Regency is the period when the Prince of Wales (later George IV) acted as regent during his father's spell of insanity 1811 – 1820). The architecture of the time was subject to overseas influences. Buildings were adorned with superficial decoration but were more delicate than had been the 18ᵗʰ century norm. The use of decorative ironwork, such as in staircases, balconies, window embellishments and railings, is a distinctive feature of this time. Curved bow windows were introduced in domestic residences.

Victorian

This was the style of architecture used in England during the reign of Queen Victoria 1841 – 1901. It was characterised by its massive construction and elaborate ornamentation. It used many different styles such as classical, Romanesque and gothic. The 'villa' was introduced and was usually semi-detached. Bow windows continued to be used but they differed from those of Regency times by having three straight sides instead of the curve.

Edwardian

Edwardian denotes the style of architecture during the reign of Edward VIIth (1901-1910). One of the features it is known for is a projecting oriel window over the front door.

People and Ranks

Peers

Peers are members of the nobility or aristocracy. A peer could be created and hold a title in his own right or it could be a courtesy title passed on to the son of a peer. Therefore it could be bestowed or inherited. The male members of the peerage (and now the female) were allowed a seat in the House of Lords. A baron was the lowest rank in the hereditary peerage and from the time of Henry 3rd the barons were summoned to parliament. The 'pecking order' of rank is Duke, Marquess, Earl, Viscount and Baron.

Any male peer is referred to as 'Lord' and any woman of the peerage is called 'Lady,' except the Duke and his wife who are referred to as Duke and Duchess.

Knights and Baronets

They are titles bestowed without the privileges of peerage or a seat in the House of Lords. 'Sir' is the title of honour placed before the name of a knight. The female equivalent is 'Dame'. The wife of a knight may be called 'Lady'. Bestowed knighthoods are not passed on.

A Baronet will have received his title from the king and this could be passed on through the direct male heir. He would be addressed as 'Sir'.

Gentleman

A term first used in the fifteenth century as a status between a baronet and a yeoman. From the sixteenth century a distinction was made between a gentleman and a yeoman to do with their way of life. A gentleman did not work with his hands and so his household included servants. Members of the professions were regarded as gentlemen.

Esquire or squire

Originally an esquire was a shield bearer to a knight. In the sixteenth century he was an officer of the crown. During the seventeenth and eighteenth centuries he did not have a title but was likely to have a coat of arms. A squire became a common term for the Lord of the Manor or the main landowner. An esquire was a superior gentleman and in the nineteenth century the term esquire became more widely used when addressing letters to a gentleman. Today it can refer to all men.

Yeoman

Yeoman is a word for a man who was a free tenant, often a farmer. Because he worked with his hands he could not be called a gentleman, but his status was higher than most other tenants. He was 'working class' in the true sense of the word and would work with his employees. He could serve on juries and vote in county elections. Later the term was used to denote a small or medium farmer.

Acknowledgements and Resources

A great deal of detailed information has been put together in this book and it has been gathered by the authors from a very wide range of sources. In what is intended to be a popular book, it would be inappropriate to provide exhaustive references for all the facts cited but wherever information is open to question or doubt the authors have tried to make this clear. It is hoped that in due course it will be possible for detailed references to be put onto the Langford History Group web-site. For the moment, though, editors and authors would wish to acknowledge and thank the many individuals who have shared their memories, those who have made available the title deeds to their properties and the various organisations that have allowed us to use their resources.

The Editors wish to thank:

all the individual authors without whom this book would not have been possible;

Max Kolombos who set up a web site for us and composed the book;

Stefan Marjoram who designed the cover and took the photographs of the houses as they are today;

Sue Shaw for her encouragement and guidance, and for visiting and verifying architectural details of individual houses;

Stan Croker for making available his collection of postcards and photographs;

Richard Dunn for his advice and help with mapping.

The assistance and recollections of several longstanding Langford residents have been especially valuable. Particular thanks are due to **Beatrice Berry**, **Stan & Gill Croker**, **Jean Darby**, **Polly King** and **Ernest Morris**.

Somerset Record Office has provided tithe apportionment maps and schedules for Burrington and Churchill parishes, and has been the source of many of the individual documents used. Much data has been obtained from the Kelly's Directories and other resources held in the North Somerset Studies Centre at Weston-super-Mare Library. The Register of Listed Buildings is held by North Somerset Council Planning Department. Census returns were obtained from the National Archives. The Dictionary of National Biography has provided information on a few of the more eminent residents of Langford.

Cartographic information has been provided by the Ordnance Survey and the chapter on Langford in Maps benefited from accessing this data through the Digimap Historical Mapping database provided by EDINA.

Previous publications on the history of the local area that have been particularly valuable include:

Butler, W. F., *Churchill People and Places*, (2003);

Croker, S., *Picture Postcards of the Early 1900s – The Wrington Vale*, (2005);

Fryer, J., *Looking Back at Langford: an illustrated history of the village*, (Woodspring Resource Centre, 2001);

Hodges, M. A., *Churchill: a brief history*, (1994);

Llewellyn, E. H., *Burrington*, (1911);

Marsden-Smedley, C., *Burrington, Church and Village, a short history*, (1991);

Also, John Bailey's articles in the Weston Mercury and the book produced for European Architectural Heritage Year – 1975, by Burrington W.I. and Langford W.I.

The help provided by the following for individual chapters is gratefully acknowledged:

Langford Court:	Martin Llewellyn for the portraits of former occupiers; The Woodland Trust Report on Dolebury Warren;
Lodge Farm:	Gena Williams, Jane Bell and Julian Wills;
Rose Cottage:	Peter Evans for photographs;
Dring Cottage:	Sally Greenhill;
Milfort/Hylesbroke:	Paul & Alison Norcross, Meg Buxton, Steve Hale, Betty Jefferies, Sylvia Norton, Audrey Plumley, Rose Jessen, Dr. Trevor Shaw OBE, Rosemary Johnson, Sarah Virjee;
Wistaria House:	Hazel Sturgis;
Devonshire House:	Paul Gardner;
York Cottage:	Dudley Lewis and Bridget Woolstone;
Richmond House:	Sally Logie.

Index